The Supplemental Guide to Fun and Social Travel

Now this is Life.™

PUBLISHED BY PARTYEARTH™ LLC

The PartyEarth team would like to thank Jesse Jachman and Michael Kovach. Without their hard work, creativity, and energy, this book would not have been possible. The team would also like to express gratitude to Lee Hickman and Gecko Studios, Brent Vincent, and Matt Wilson for their contributions to the book.

Copyright © 2006 by PartyEarth™ LLC

Printed in the United States by Banta Company. No part of this book may be reproduced or transmitted without the express written consent of PartyEarth LLC, except in the case of brief quotations embodied in reviews or critical articles.

PartyEarth™ and Now THIS is Life™ are trademarks of PartyEarth LLC.

For inquiries, suggestions, corrections, volume purchase discounts, and more, please visit us at www.partyeurope.com or www.partyearth.com.

ISBN: 0-9761120-2-7

Disclaimers: The authors and publisher of this book did everything possible to provide accurate information. The data presented represents their best available information at the time of publication. All commentary in this book is meant to be opinion, not fact, and all tips are the authors' points of view. The "reviewers" (Tucker, Adam, Brittney, and Emma) are fictitious, and any resemblance to actual persons, living or dead, is purely coincidental. Additionally, PartyEarth accepts no responsibility for injuries, illnesses, property damage, fines or incarcerations incurred while using this book. Use your best judgment when traveling, and whenever unclear about the legality or safety of something presented in this book, ask the local authorities. Be smart, be safe, be respectful of the locals and their customs, and have the time of your life.

CONTENTS

How to 'Party London & Paris'

Party London & Paris - The Concept   p. 1

Meet the Reviewers   p. 2

How to Use Party London & Paris   p. 7

Where Do You Want to Party Today?

London   p. 10

Paris   p. 60

THE CONCEPT

Imagine that before leaving for London & Paris, you could send your best friend ahead of you to scout out the most fun and social things to do. This friend understands your personality - your likes, dislikes, and moods - and has a knack for figuring out where to be and when. He is able, therefore, to recommend the spots that you would most enjoy in all of your varying moods. Now imagine that this friend wrote a book conveying all of this information in an easily accessible format. In a nutshell - that's Party London & Paris!

The Perfect Supplement to the Comprehensive Guides
(Let's Go!, Lonely Planet, Rough Guides, etc.)

The all-inclusive guides are excellent resources to help you navigate through London & Paris, find places to eat and stay that fit your budget, and make sure you know the sights to see. But because they cover so much, they can't provide depth in an extremely critical area, an area on which most young travelers focus - ways to simply have fun. Party London & Paris was created to fill this void. With this book in your hands, you will find that no matter where you are, what day it is, how you feel, or who you are with, you will know where and how to have the maximum amount of fun possible.

Hundreds of Detailed Reviews of Fun and Social Day and Night Places in London & Paris' Hottest Destinations

Because fun means something different to everyone, you need choices, and you need variety. With hundreds of reviews, we uncover a myriad of the most vibrant and interesting social venues in London & Paris - and not just bars and clubs (although we cover them thoroughly). We also review parks, beaches, plazas, neighborhoods, hostels, restaurants, and other venues provided they are especially fun and social. Our reviews not only cover all of the basics - address, hours, prices, hot nights, and the scene, but they also offer savvy advice and rankings. Our mission is simply to ensure that you find the coolest ways to idle away your days and the hottest spots to spend your nights.

The Best of the Best

As the authority on fun and social travel, we want to narrow the choices for you while still offering plenty of options. With thousands of hangouts and festivities to choose from, we must focus our review process on the best of the best places in London & Paris. Whether it is the wealth of beers on tap, the funky atmosphere, the hip clientele, the beat on the dance floor, or the hospitality, we maintain that we bring you THE most fun and social venues for a wide variety of tastes. We also seek to validate the reputations of well-known and highly praised spots. We work hard/party hard to provide both the breadth and depth of information that will empower you to chose what scene is best for you at any given time.

Make Every Day and Night Count - Can You Afford Not To?

We understand the investment you are making in your trip, and we know that you probably can't afford the time and expense of uninformed decisions, so having the right information is paramount. Imagine arriving in an amazing city like London on a Tuesday night knowing that you only have a night or two before you have to head off to Paris. Tuesday nights can be difficult to find a hot spot - unless of course you're carrying Party London & Paris. With detailed choices by day of the week, you'll know the best places to hit on typically "off" nights. After all, you don't want to find yourself wandering the streets "in search of" when you can be "living it up". So, for the cost of one cover charge in a European club, Party London & Paris will enable you to squeeze every last ounce of fun out of your time abroad. Your investment will be matched many times over in these pages. Simply put, you can't afford not to have this book.

The Complete Package

What you get with the purchase of this book, however, goes beyond advice, reviews, and ratings. You gain access to a community of young travelers who, like you, are looking for a good time. **www.Partyeurope.com** enables you to find a partner in crime, to give us your opinion of a spot we cover, or to suggest additional hot spots and hangouts. We are building a dialogue among young travelers, and we think you all have something to contribute. Our message board will put you in touch with other travelers who might want to share some of their wisdom or who are looking for fellow young travelers to meet up with and explore all of London & Paris' greatest pleasures.

Whoever you are and whatever your scene, if you're in search of a good time, we'll lead you to it. With Party London & Paris in your pocket, consider yourself an empowered traveler about to have the most incredible time of your life.

THE REVIEWERS

Who do we think we are…claiming to know your scene and to understand what you might like to do while traveling in Europe? We have assembled a team of 4 individuals who represent a spectrum of young travelers, encompassing a variety of moods, tastes, and perspectives. Each traveler is meant to characterize aspects of you and your friends, so that you might identify with a traveler or two and heed their advice as you make your way through Europe.You can even visit our website at PartyEarth.com and complete a survey to determine who you are most like and how closely your tastes match each traveler's. This should help you narrow your choices of fun and social venues, as you can pay particular attention to the suggestions of the traveler(s) who most closely resemble(s) you.

Who are they?

They're you - or some combination of them is you. They're young, adventurous, hip or not, crazy or calm, sometimes saving, sometimes splurging, bold or apprehensive, energetic or just looking to chill on the beach with a bottle of wine, impeccably dressed or hangin' out in a t-shirt and Birks...ALWAYS in the mood for a good time. Tucker, Adam, Brittany, and Emma are you in your varying moods and with your diverse tastes. Together, they'll give you the down and dirty on their favorite haunts, and each of them will assess every place. Whether you are looking for leisure or festivity, they'll help you make the most of your time in London & Paris.

So that you might get to know them better, we asked a few questions of each of our 4 travelers. So, here's the scoop on Tucker, Adam, Brittney, and Emma.

TUCKER:

Tucker is a semi-preppy, beer-drinking fraternity boy (in all the best senses of the word). He prefers a bar to a club any day, especially if it's packed with pretty girls. Laid-back and fun loving, Tuck is entertained by good conversation or good music in the simplest of bars. He is out to make some amazing memories while in Europe, so he's willing to try anything. • **Can't leave home without:** His backwards baseball cap • **Favorite drink:** Anything in a keg • **Favorite Movie:** Old School • **Favorite Place to Be:** Barcelona • **Turn-ons:** Mini-skirts • **Favorite Show:** Sportscenter • **For fun I:** Drink beers in a sports bar while catching the big game • **Favorite European experience:** The Running of the Bulls • **What I look for in a travel companion:** Someonewho likes to party. They should have a head on their shoulders but be willing to experiment, be laid back but always down to get a little crazy.

ADAM:

Don't expect to find Adam dressed up to go out - ever. This laid back, earthy, hippy-type is happy just to chill and be. Whether it is lounging in a beautiful park, exploring off the beaten path, or seeking out unique vistas, Adam is engaged by a quirky and unusual scene. He prefers a more casual, eclectic, even crunchy venue where he can meet interesting new people, listen to great music, and simply hang out while taking in a distinctive vibe. • **Can't leave the country without:** Visine • **What's on my IPOD:** Phish and The Dead • **For fun I:** toss a Frisbee and jam on the guitar • **Favorite body part:** the earlobe • **Favorite movie:** Dazed and Confused • **Bar, club, pub, or park:** Definitely park • **Favorite European city:** Amsterdam • **Where I want to go next:** Cinque Terre • **Philosophy on travel:** Perpetuate it…everybody should always be traveling throughout the course of their life…don't go somewhere just to knock it off your list of places to see…go somewhere to become a part of the culture for a day/week/month or more… be a sponge and absorb/integrate what you learn from your travels.

BRITTNEY:

The epitome of a city girl, Brittney wants to be at THE place to be, the hottest and hippest nightclub or lounge. Dressed to kill and with the energy to match, you'll often find her closing down the clubs by night and shopping as only she knows how by day.

• **Favorite accessory:** Her designer clutch • **Favorite 80's tune:** Tiffany- "I think we're alone now" • **Can't leave home without:** my credit card • **Favorite European City:** London • **What I want to do most this year:** Meet someone who can put up with me. • **Favorite Workout:** Pilates • **Biggest risk I've ever taken:** A wet t-shirt contest in front of thousands in Cancun • **Pet Peeve:** People who insist on having boring conversations with me • **Turn-ons:** Well put together guys with a sense of style • **Favorite Reality TV show:** Nip/Tuck • **Why I love to travel:** It's such an incredible opportunity to experience places that are completely vibrant and alive and others that are so laid back. I love being exposed to the fashion, the styles, the shopping, the parties, and the different paces of life. It's a rush to try new things and see places that are so unlike home.

EMMA:

The lively and sociable girl next door, Emma is happy doing anything and everything, from clubbing and dancing, to chilling with a beer and shooting pool, to hiking. She'll find something to enjoy in just about any setting, as long as it doesn't cost a fortune. Emma is traveling on a tight budget, and it is this fact alone that restricts her interests. • **Biggest Vice:** Tequila Shots • **Movie I've seen most:** Ferris Bueller's Day Off • **Favorite Athlete:** Mia Hamm • **Favorite European Destination:** Rome • **What I look for in a travel companion:** Someone who is fun, social, caring, and somewhat down to earth. • **What I want to do most this year:** Finish school and get settled into a job that enables me to help others. • **Favorite body part:** eyes • **Can't leave home without:** The picture of my family in my wallet • **Philosophy on travel:** Get out and see what the world has to offer. Don't get trapped in American ways of life without first seeing how those in other parts of the world live. Take pictures and keep a diary to remember amazing experiences down the road.

HOW TO USE PARTY LONDON & PARIS

Each city's chapter brings together the raw material on every chosen venue and our travelers' opinions, rankings, and advice. Our experience and its honest portrayal in the pages of this book should enable you to become easily acclimated to each city, establish realistic and outrageously fun expectations, and prioritize your activities in order to get the most out of each day and night you have to spend. So many questions and decisions will arise as you plan your trip and as you travel, questions that go unanswered in every other travel guide. Party London & Paris is designed specifically to answer those questions. Each section that we have included in the city chapters serves the very distinct purpose of doing just that.

How should I prioritize which cities to go to and how long to spend in each?

- **The Party Climate:** This section captures the highlights of the city's social scene so that you can prepare yourself for the best of what lies ahead. By understanding the flavor of each city's frivolity, you can determine whether you will include a destination in your trip, how much time you will spend there, and how you will spend that time, in general. You'll arrive in the city understanding what it has to offer, without being overwhelmed by the details. Knowing whether you are about to hit a casual bar town, a swanky club scene, a backpacker's paradise, beer garden central, or, in many cases, a wonderfully diverse combination of these will enable you to arrive there knowing what to expect and, therefore, to make the most of it.

- **Our Overall Impressions:** Each traveler will give his or her general take on the fun to be had in the city. Having identified with one or more of these travelers, you can get a more focused picture of how that city will suit you on a broad level.

If I have only one day to spend in a city, what should I do?

- **Our Perfect Days/Nights:** An intense look at the very best the city has to offer, this segment indicates the venues you can't miss depending on your personality, mood, and tastes. Each traveler has selected his/her favorite spots to hit during the day and night, and the traveler who most liked the city provides a detailed itinerary for a perfect day and night there. Again, focus on the traveler(s) most like you for insight into the best of the best. These are the places we are passionate about.

If I have several days to spend in a city, what could I do?

- **Our Top 5 Spots:** If your time is short and/or you want every minute in a city to be intense, take note of each traveler's 5 favorite fun and social places. Here, you'll find each city's best diversions, making your choices infinitely easier.

It's a random Tuesday night, where should I go?

- **Hotspots by Night of the Week:** This is the scoop on where to be every night of the week, so you'll know where to head even on typically "off" nights. No more wandering the streets on a quiet weeknight wondering if anything is going on and if you'll find it. So, whether it takes you off the beaten path or allows you to try out someone else's scene for a change, this chart depicts the low down for each traveler each night.

I'm going out in this great neighborhood, what can I expect from the social scene here?

- **Neighborhoods/The Social Landscape:** Understanding the social identity of neighborhoods and how they are oriented within the city will enable you to acclimate to each city more quickly and to focus your planning on areas most suited for you. Again, our goal is to eliminate time wasted searching for a good time.

I'm looking for something great to do today/tonight, where should I go?

- **Reviews:** This is the meat, the particulars, where to go, what to expect when you get there, what to wear, how much it will cost you, and a tip from the crew member who liked each place the most. You'll find just enough of these for each city to offer variety, but not so much as to overwhelm you. From the moment you arrive, you'll know what's available and how to access it.
- Pay particular attention to the **travelers' heads**; Tucker, Adam, Brittney, and Emma will grant each place 0-4 heads based on how well it fulfills his/her particular likes and needs. Once you know who shares your preferences, you can choose and dismiss places based on their recommendations.

---
4 - Do whatever you can to check this place out
3 - You'll love it
2 - You'll have fun
1 - Only go in a bind
0 - Avoid like the plague

- **The tip from one of our travelers**, which is an essential part of every review, will give you a more personal insight into these venues.

With Party London & Paris in hand, you'll be equipped with the information you need to make great decisions about the fun you'll have. We think you'll agree that we've distilled the social scene in these European cities down to only the best places, while still ensuring that whatever your personality, your mood, your budget, or the area of town in which you find yourself, there will be fun to be had by you.

How to read a Review

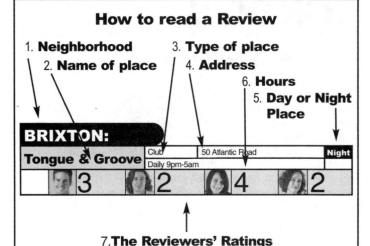

1. **Neighborhood**
2. **Name of place**
3. **Type of place**
4. **Address**
5. **Day or Night Place**
6. **Hours**
7. **The Reviewers' Ratings**

The Scene One of the best-kept secrets in London, Tongue and Groove is a small, very intimate lounge/club where all visitors are invited and greatly appreciated. Red-painted walls and large black couches provide the backdrop for this compact club. With not a lot of room to spread out, people find any place to dance including the tops of speakers, and the DJ is relegated to an area practically on the dance floor. What really sets T&G apart is that the people go out of their way to be welcoming and friendly, making it one of the best places in London to meet people. **Crowd** Some of the hippest people in Brixton and all over London come here to dance and hang out all night. Lots of media types frequent this spot as well. The crowd is upper 20s to 30s, very friendly and not pretentious at all. The people here want to get away from the exclusivity of the posh Chelsea and West End clubs.
Entertainment/Music Tongue and Groove actually gets some very famous DJs form all over the world. They love to play here, because they feel like part of the crowd. The music is mostly techno but not hardcore at all. **Prices** Beers £3, mixed drinks £4.50, cover charge at the door starts at £3, can be a little higher depending on the night and how crowded. **Dress** Somewhat dressy, but Brixton is never as fancy.
Hot Nights/When to Go Late night spot, but go around 12-2:30am to avoid the line and get a spot to chill for the night.

8. **The Particulars of Each Venue**

Tip from Brittney: "This place is totally worth the trip to Brixton. Get here around 12 and just hang out the rest of the night on a big comfy couch. The people here are so friendly and the mood is so lively, you'll want to stay here all night."

9. **Tip from Reviewer**

LONDON

The Party Climate:

London's social scene is one of distinct choices. It offers a daytime drinking culture in which locals gather at the pub after work, grab pints with some friends, and head home happy at 11pm when the pubs close. At the same time, London is host to crazy, hip clubs (like Fabric) where some of the world's most popular DJs keep the dance floors thumping until 6 or 7am. As a traveler, you will have no trouble accessing the frivolity of either of these choices, provided you arrive at the clubs looking good and on the early side. (Despite spacious interiors, huge bouncers love to make you feel small, so just patiently wait your turn...you'll get in.)

It is easy to meet people in these pubs, bars, and clubs, since folks speak English, though proper, and are friendly and welcoming of Americans. Cultural adjustments are minimal, so blending in and having a great time are a given here. This is not to say that you won't encounter the occasional stiff upper lip.

In contrast to the relatively casual, easy atmosphere among London's pubs, bars, and clubs, there is also a side to London's nightlife to which few are guaranteed access. At these exclusive clubs, if you don't show up in a BMW, dressed in a suit, and ready to throw down the credit card, you better be with someone who is. If you aren't on the guest list and aren't a pretty girl or with a pretty girl, your chances are slim, and pleading with the bouncer is about as useful as your mandatory freshman writing class. This is a scene for those who appreciate the finer things that abound in London's elite circles, but if you can figure a way in, you won't regret it.

Daytime in London offers its own variety of things to do with spectacular parks and great shopping. Hyde and Regent's Parks are among the most beautiful and peaceful you will ever find, and they provide a perfect refuge in which to recover from the frenzied nightlife. And Harrods, though outrageously expensive, can provide hours of browsing and people-watching to fill your day.

When making your partying plans in London, remember that the energy here flows from the local pubs during the week (and during the day) and from the insane clubs on the weekend nights. Just be sure to save up, because a couple of nights of partying in London could put you in a bind financially. Nevertheless, you can save some money and energy in a park by day and relish the myriad of social venues providing action after dark.

Our Overall Impressions:

Tucker - 3

"I really like the pub scene here, because they do know their beer in London. It seems like every corner has a pub with tons of great beers on tap, which is awesome. The only problem is they all close up at 11pm, and I'm just getting going. London's bars and clubs, however, are easy spots to meet people (especially girls), because everyone speaks English and is so friendly."

Adam - 3

"Although it's known for its posh clubs (and you know that's just not me), London has so much more to offer. There is a scene suited for just about anyone here. With so much good live music every night, I know that I won't find myself bored anytime soon. I also really love London's beautiful parks for whiling away the daytime hours. And the markets...amazing. Definitely no shortage of places to chill out and take in a different vibe here."

Brittney - 4

"There is pretty much nothing that I dislike about London. This city offers the most upscale stores and some of the best shopping I have ever seen. Very cosmopolitan! Let me just say that I freaked out when I saw Harrods. And the clubs ...unbelievable. Londoners seem to have great taste in everything...cars, jewelry, clothes. I could spend so much time here, like my life. I'd love a flat in Kensington or Chelsea. This is truly my kind of city."

Emma - 3

"Even though London is quite possibly the most expensive city in the world, you don't necessarily have to have a trust fund to have a good time here. You just need to think a little more about how you spend your time and money. So many bars offer great Happy hour deals, and some pubs have really reasonably priced drinks. The only problem is that almost every bar has a cover charge (though you can sometimes squeeze in early before they start charging), and the clubs are very expensive. The daytime here is another thing entirely...so much to do for nothing. With beautiful parks for hanging out and people watching and plenty of browsing at the many shopping venues, I can really spend some time here and stay on my budget."

Our Perfect Days/Nights:

Brittney:
"Like I said, I could really see myself living here, basking in the club scene, shopping, and just appreciating the class and sophistication that London exemplifies. But if I had only a single day, I know exactly how I'd spend it. After sleeping late, I'd spend a couple of hours wandering around **Harrods**, browsing and splurging. I'd run by the food court for a quick bite and some coffee before meeting friends and taking the tube down to London Bridge, where we will hit **Vinopolis** for a wine tasting tour. Since it's still early, I'll take the premium tour…along with a shot of absinthe, of course. This will take a couple of hours, so I'll surely be hungry when it's over. The **Wine Wharf** next to Vinopolis is convenient, but on a nice night I want to go to **Cantina del Ponte** for a delicious Italian dinner of wine and risotto on the river. As the sun sets, it is time to pre-game with the hip London crowd at **Eclipse**. Just taking in the sophisticated scene and sipping a watermelon martini puts me in the mood for a rowdy night. I'm sure that the crowd here is heading over to **Boujis** later, so that is where I'll be too. I'll gather my energy by relaxing on a posh couch in the corner before hitting the fantastic dance floor. I know, it's been a long day, but my friends and I want to keep the party going, so we'll grab a taxi and head to Fabric until 7am. Maybe some nice guy will invite me into the VIP room so I don't have to deal with the huge crowd here. I don't know if I'd survive it, but, wow, what a day that would be."

Tucker:
Day - Premiership Soccer Match, Regent's Park
Night - Roadhouse, Boujis, Fabric, Vingt Quatre

Adam:
Day- Camden Town Market, Regent's Park
Night - Dublin Castle, Fabric, Maroush

Emma:
Day - Portobello Market, Hyde Park
Night - The World's End, Los Locos, Bar Italia

Our Top 5 Spots:

Tucker
1. Boujis
2. Soccer Match
3. Roadhouse
4. Fabric
5. Zoo Bar

Adam
1. Camden Market
2. Fabric
3. Alphabet
4 Dublin Castle
5. Regent's Park

Brittney
1. Boujis
2. Harrods
3. Fabric
4. Eclipse
5. Vinopolis

Emma
1. Hyde Park
2. The World's End
3. Walkabout
4. Ye Olde Chesire Cheese
5. Harrods

Hotspots by Night of the Week:

	Mon	Tu	Wed	Th	F	Sa	Su
	Zoo Bar	Gardening Club	The O'Bar	Tiger Tiger	Roadhouse /Boujis (if you can get in)	Fabric	Church, Backpacker, Walkabout (all day, in that order)
	Water Rats	Dublin Castle	Café Boheme	Alphabet	The World's End	Fabric	Church, Backpacker, Walkabout (all day, in that order)
	The Langley	Bed	Alphabet	Raffles	Boujis	Fabric	Eclipse
	Open Air Theater	Alphabet	Walk about in King's Cross	Ye Olde Chesire Cheese	The World's End	Los Locos	Bed

Neighborhoods -
The Social Landscape:

Brixton: (South London)
One of the most diverse neighborhoods in London, with a large population from the West Indies, Brixton has, of late, become a hip and trendy area for those who want to escape posh and exclusive Chelsea and West End spots.

This area is young, social, and alive with a great mix of bars and all night dance clubs. You'll find some of the best DJs and the friendliest people around here.

Camden Town:
Camden Town, in a nutshell, is alternative. Because it offers the cheapest housing close to school, this is a student-populated neighborhood with a strong hippie vibe. If this is your scene, you can't miss Camden Town; though beware, it does become somewhat shady late at night. The best time to check it out is on a Sunday afternoon, when you'll find it bustling with friendly folks to meet and hang out with. The hippy inspired atmosphere that prevails here and the great live music make it distinct from other London neighborhoods and a must see.

Chelsea, King's Road Area: (tubes: Knightsbridge, Slone Square, South Kensington) London's upper class calls this neighborhood home, so it exudes sophistication and class. The clubs are posh, expensive, and exclusive, many with members only policies, so you have to be on a guest list during the weekend. Londoners here have plenty of money, and they know how to have a good time - a great combination. Champagne and top-shelf liquor flow at the night spots, and if you can get in, these places can be some of the most fun in London. Enjoy this friendly party crowd, and don't be intimidated if you don't have a Benz waiting for you at the youth hostel.

Holborn: (Farringdon Tube and Holborn Tube)
Although this is a small area, it deserves its own explanation, because it is less of a tourist attraction than the West End. There are some great, quaint little bars and pubs to check out, but they are all just a prelude to late night at ***Fabric***.

King's Cross: (King's Cross Tube)
This young and social neighborhood offers lots of fun bars and nightclubs, though some are hard to find because they were built in old freight depots. Because this isn't one of London's more expensive areas, residents are young, and the vibe is alternative (though not to the extent of Camden Town). This is a popular weekend destination for Northern London suburbanites.

Notting Hill:
An upscale neighborhood with a liberal, artsy flair and a pseudo-hippie flavor, Notting Hill has much to offer in the way of art and live music. Bars and clubs have an artistic feel, and the ***Notting Hill Arts Club*** (by the tube stop, a must see for any artist) is known for bringing up some of the best local bands. Without a doubt, the best time to visit Notting Hill is on a Saturday afternoon for the ***Portobello Market***.

West End (the center of London Tourism, encompasses Piccadilly, Leicester Square, Covent Garden, Oxford Circus, and Tottenham Court): By far the most tourist-laden area of London, the West End offers huge, eye-catching clubs and a rowdy scene. The clubs and bars around here are a blast, though a little expensive (all have cover charges). The pubs do not, but they all close up disappointingly early - 11pm. Local Londoners tend to avoid this area in general, but you may run into some at the exclusive clubs on West End side streets...if you can find them. These venues have small signs, presumably so as not to attract hordes of tourists. If you are searching for London's hottest nightlife, you'll find it here.

BRIXTON:

Dogstar

Bar	389 Coldharbour Lane	**Night**
S-Th 12pm-2 am, F-Sa 12pm-4am		

2   3   2   3

The Scene Although it looks like a traditional pub from the outside, Dogstar is something completely different. The large, sparsely decorated space is dominated by a dance floor, which is transformed nightly into a vibrant club. With wicked light shows and huge speakers that thump to the beats of local DJ talent, this scene is fun yet casual. Music here rotates nightly between funk, electric, hip-hop, and reggae. If you are interested in just chilling out and catching up with friends, leather couches along the wall and the tiny beer garden patio out back provide ample space for that. **Crowd** The crowd ranges from mid-20s to 30s. In general, the clubs in Brixton attract hip yet unpretentious patrons who want to focus on the music and not who they are or what they look like. **Entertainment/Music** DJ every night of the week. Genre varies nightly from electric to funk to reggae to hip-hop **Food/Misc** No food here, but plenty of cocktails with names referencing sex (like the screaming orgasm) **Prices** Cover charge £3 before 11pm, £5 after; beers start at £2.80, mixed drinks £3.30. **Web Site** www.dogstar.com **Dress** Smart casual, though no strict dress code. **Hot Nights/When to Go** At its best on the weekends around midnight

Tip from Emma: "Every club in London has a cover charge, but the one at the Dogstar is not as bad. Also with cheap drinks compared to the rest, I can come here all night, not have to worry as much about money, and just have a good time."

Fridge

Club	1 Town Hall Parade	**Night**
F and Sa opens at 10pm, can stay open until 12pm		

2   1   3   1

The Scene This former theater is very unassuming from the outside, but not at all within. The walls bear remnants of fine wood paneling and leftover theater décor, but the darkness of this venue makes it difficult to notice. This hard trance techno club lays claim to one of the best light shows in London. The heart of Fridge is a gigantic dance floor encircled by a balcony providing a great perspective of the action below. There are plenty of dark hallways and side-rooms providing calmer, smaller areas to take a break from the trance, as well as smaller rooms with more chill techno. Fridge is a destination for hardcore ravers. (No association with the Fridge Bar). **Crowd** A young, wired crowd who is serious about their techno. Also, alternates between a gay and straight club. Most of the crowd here is also going to be on some type of drug to keep them going into the early morning. **Entertainment/Music** Hardcore trance from the moment you walk in and very loud. **Prices** Cover charge can be up to £10, depending on when you come. Drinks start at £3.30. **Dress** Whatever a hardcore raver would wear, but no dress code really enforced here. **Hot Nights/When to Go** If at all, go here late when everything else in Brixton is closed.

Tip from Tuck: "Everything else in Brixton is closed, and you want to keep the night going. Go to the Fridge and check out the scene. Remember, it alternates between a gay and straight club."

Fridge Bar

Bar	1 Town Hall Parade	**Night**
	M-Th open until 2am, Fr-Sa until 4:30am, Su until 3am	

👤 2 👤 3 👤 2 👤 2

LONDONBRIXTON

The Scene The Fridge Bar is reminiscent of a basement that has been pimped out to take you back to the 1970s. The décor and atmosphere are vibrant and include a narrow bar with blue and green rectangles blended in and disco balls of varying sizes hanging from the ceiling. However, there is nothing 1970s about the music. The focus here is strictly hip-hop and reggae - no techno, drum, bass, or any of that. A larger dance floor downstairs allows the dance party to break out. **Crowd** Local Brixton folk frequent this spot, primarily to sip cocktails. Once in a while, they break it out and go down to the dance floor. **Entertainment/Music** Monday: roots reggae and dub, Tuesday: salsa night with a live salsa band and dance lessons, Wednesday: Old-school Reggae, Thursday: Miami Bass and R&B, Friday: Hip-hop and R&B, Saturday: More hip-hop, Sunday: Old-school classics. **Food/Misc** This place no longer has their chill out early morning from 5:30-11am. Turned out to be lots of fighting and not so chill. **Prices** No cover M-Th, Fr: free before 10:30pm, £5 11pm, £7 before 12am, £10 after 12am. Sa: same as Fr. Su: £5 after 10:30pm, £3 with flyer. Beers £3.20, mixed drink £3.50. **Dress** Smart casual **Hot Nights/When to Go** The weekend gets the most crowded, when they have reggae music.

Tip from Adam: "The upstairs is the best place to meet people, and this place will let you meet a different crowd from the rest of London's social scene. The nights they play reggae are the ones I like best."

Living

Club	443 Coldharbour Ln	**Night**
	M-Th 5pm-2am, F 5pm-4am, Sa 12pm-4am, Su 12pm-2am	

👤 3 👤 1 👤 3 👤 2

The Scene Living has very much a lounge-like feel with ultra-modern ergonomic chairs, funky tables, and brown leather couches. You will be struck immediately by the colorful glow in the club contributed by the constant projected lights spinning around the room. The upstairs and downstairs offer completely different music, depending on the night - anything goes. You might hear hits from the 80s and 90s, hip-hop, or any other genre (except for Country). The DJ is the main attraction, as the patrons here like to dance. Some come just to chill out for the night. **Crowd** This club attracts some of Brixton's more hip and young crowds, as they like the feel of the sofas and the beats. There is also an alternative look amongst the patrons with funky hairstyles and t-shirts. Early in the night, there is a strong contingency of Brixton's West Indian population. **Entertainment/Music** A DJ on both floors. The music here changes every night, but the main focus is hip-hop, drum, bass, and pop. **Prices** Cover: Fr- free before 10pm, £5 after 10pm, £2 if on the guest list; Sa- free before 10pm, £5 before 11pm, £7 after 11pm. £2.50 shots. Cocktails start at £5.50, beers £3, mixed drinks £4.50 **Web Site** www.livingbar.co.uk **Dress** A smart casual dress code, but not as fancy as Soho clubs **Hot Nights/When to Go** This place can get crowded any night. A good idea to get here before 12 to avoid a line, though you will still be here a while.

Tip from Tuck: "A lounge type place is not always for me, but I can come here early and mix with the unique Brixton crowd. I like to stay here late, because I can keep it interesting by switching up floors to get a different vibe. Also, some very nice-looking approachable girls are among the crowd."

Satay Bar

Restaurant/Bar	447-455 Coldharbour Ln	Night
M-Th 12-11pm, F 12-2am, Sa 1pm-2am, Su 1pm-11pm		

2 3 2 3

The Scene The tremendous blend of aromas from the Indian cuisine and incense put you at ease as you walk into Satay. With its relaxed drum and bass beats, Satay is one of the most chill bars in all of Brixton. Walls decorated with modern West Indian art and golden-glowing mini chandeliers add to the soothing atmosphere. Around 10:30pm on the weekends, the restaurant closes down, and music takes over. **Crowd** A majority are West Indians from Brixton. **Entertainment/Music** DJs playing chill and relaxed music Friday and Saturday nights until 2am. **Food/Misc** A full Indian menu served until 11pm **Prices** Happy hour (everyday 5-8pm): £3.50 cocktails, £10 jugs; very reasonable meals start at £5.95, £3 beers, £4.50 mix drinks, £3 cover after 11pm. **Web Site** www.sataybar.co.uk **Dress** Smart casual **Hot Nights/When to Go** Weekends after 11pm for music, but before 11 for food. Best idea is to start your night here, then move on to another bar in Brixton.

Tip from Emma: "The food here is very good, so come early for dinner and mix with the very open and personable crowd. If you want a laid back night, your best bet is to stay here. Otherwise, this place is great way to start off a night in Brixton."

Tongue and Groove

Club	50 Atlantic Road	Night
Daily 9pm-5am		

3 2 4 2

The Scene One of the best-kept secrets in London, Tongue and Groove is a small, very intimate lounge/club where all visitors are welcome and greatly appreciated. Red-painted walls and large black couches provide the backdrop for this compact club. Without a lot of room to spread out, people find any place to dance, including the tops of speakers, and the DJ is relegated to an area practically on the dance floor. What really sets T&G apart is that the people go out of their way to be welcoming and friendly, making it one of the best places in London to meet people. **Crowd** Some of the hippest people in Brixton and all over London come here to dance and hang out all night. Lots of media types frequent this spot as well. The crowd is upper 20s to 30s, very friendly and not pretentious at all. The people here want to get away from the exclusivity of the posh Chelsea and West End clubs. **Entertainment/Music** Tongue and Groove actually gets some very famous DJs from all over the world. They love to play here, because they feel like part of the crowd. The music is mostly techno but not hardcore at all. **Prices** Beers £3, mixed drinks £4.50, cover charge at the door starts at £3, can be a little higher depending on the night and how crowded **Dress** Somewhat dressy, but Brixton is never as fancy **Hot Nights/When to Go** Late night spot, but go around 12-12:30am to avoid the line and get a spot to chill for the night

Tip from Brittney: "This place is totally worth the trip to Brixton. Get here around 12 and just hang out the rest of the night on a big comfy couch. The people here are so friendly and the mood is so lively, you'll want to stay here all night."

CAMDEN TOWN:

Camden Market — Shopping — Day

4   4   3   4

The Scene The people, sights, sounds, smells, and tastes of Camden Market meld into an intriguing and alternative London landscape. Punks, hippies, and other creative sorts congregate in this area to buy and sell a sundry of art, jewelry, clothes, and recreational drugs. The end of the market by the river beckons if you are hungry, with Japanese, Mexican, Moroccan, and Chinese cuisine side by side. The mellow atmosphere throughout the market seems to arise from and encourage aimless wandering, people-watching, nibbling on ethnic food, and creative self-expression. All ages and types seem attracted, at least momentarily, to this alternative vibe. Taking in all this scene has to offer will make for a great day in London. **Crowd** Truly people of all ages and walks of life. Folks here exemplify laid-back. **Entertainment/Music** Great people-watching. **Food/Misc** Ethnic foods and snacks, recreational paraphernalia. **Prices** Reasonably priced food. Approximately £4 for most meals. **Hot Nights/When to Go** Sunday afternoon. **Close By** Plenty of pubs and bars to pop into for a beer. Camden Lock, Henry J. Beans are pub-like, and Lloyd's bar is a bit upscale.

Tip from Adam: "This is a great place to just space out and pop in and out of shops or boutiques. You might even want to hit a basement coffee shop to sample that alternative scene. It's also a treat to try the wide range of ethnic foods."

The Church — Other — Kentish Town, The Forum — Only Sundays, 12pm-4:15pm — Day

4   3   3   4

The Scene Truly an extreme way to spend a Sunday afternoon in the city. The Church has the reputation of hosting some of the wildest parties in London, and anything goes here. Although it has had to relocate many times due to its rowdy nature, the party scene is still going strong in Kentish Town. Patrons here are simply letting loose and often don costumes, which only help to crank up the energy in an already raucous atmosphere. **Crowd** No hint of the classy, posh club-scene crowd here. Primarily 20-somethings out for a really crazy time. **Entertainment/Music** Dance music of all kinds. **Prices** 3 drinks for £7. **Dress** Again, anything goes; many people in costumes. **Hot Nights/When to Go** Sunday noon (right when it opens)

Tip from Emma: "Probably one of the best ways to meet people and hang out all day with them...but get here by 12, or you will have a hard time getting in."

Dublin Castle

Club	94 Parkway	**Night**
M-Sa open until 1am, Su until 12am		

  4   3   1   3

The Scene One of the best live music venues for new bands trying to make it famous. Walking in, it seems like any typical Irish pub. But in the back, you'll find a small, 150-person, standing room only, intimate concert venue where all of the action takes place. The Dublin Castle has, over the years, become an icon of the British rock scene. Tuesday nights are great for the best band showcase, but the biggest crowds come out on Friday nights. **Crowd** The type of music and area attract an indie/alternative crowd. **Entertainment/Music** There is live music here every night of the week. Three bands every night and occasionally more. **Prices** Cover £5 Su-Th, £6 F-Sa. Beers £2.90, mixed drinks £2.60. **Dress** No dress codes. Dress too well, and you will feel out of place. **Hot Nights/When to Go** Bands nightly (check "Time Out"); Tuesday nights are when they get the best bands.

Tip from Adam: "Every night the live music is great, and there's a good time to be had. What makes this place special is the likelihood that you'll see an amazing band before they really make it. You'll be able to say you saw them way back when..."

The Elephant's Head

Pub/Café	224 Camden High Street	**Night**
Pub Hours		

  2   3   1   2

The Scene A traditional British pub with a very liberal feel, the Elephant's Head is yet another spot in Camden Town where the crowd is eclectic and typically very open-minded. Patrons love to come here to get away from "boring" people at the old-fashioned pubs. Although the bar is covered in finished wood inside, which gives it the same appearance of many other pubs around the city, this pub's character is that of its crowd. Sixties music on Saturdays is always crazy, and Sunday, this pub is a good place to veg out with some reggae beats. **Crowd** Eclectic as can be…early twenties to late thirties. Weekdays around 6pm, when people get off of work, and weekends around 8/9pm are the busier times. It has a bit of a grunge feel, but don't be surprised to see some suits in here as well. **Entertainment/Music** Juke Box; Saturday, they play sixties music all night long, and the place really gets jumping. Sunday, the place fills up as they play reggae/soul music all day and night, but the scene tends to be groups of people drinking at tables and hanging out. **Food/Misc** Traditional Bar food (£5-7) **Prices** Beers £2-3, Spirits £3-5, wine for £11/12 a bottle, £3-4 a glass. **Dress** Anything goes. **Hot Nights/When to Go** Fr/Sa around 9pm or Sunday afternoon/evening.

Tip from Adam: "I'm a big fan of Camden Town in general, so this is another place I love to groove in. On Sunday, the music is hot, so I'd say stop by for a bite, a pint, and a chance to chat with some grungy all-stars."

Jazz Café

Restaurant	5 Parkway	**Night**
M-Sa 7pm-2am, Su 7pm-1am		

The Scene The upstairs balcony restaurant is chill, but the main focus here is the large live music stage. Some great Jazz, Funk, Latin, and Hip-Hop artists come to this venue, where there is a show every night of the week. As you would imagine, the scene here is largely determined by the music, which can range from mellow to something that makes the whole room bounce. On weekends, strobe lights flash and beats thump, as a myriad of people come here to dance to the Jazz Café's 'late night' sessions from 11pm-2am. **Crowd** Completely dependent on the evening's entertainment. **Entertainment/Music** Music every night - a mix of live groups and famous local DJs. **Food/Misc** An upscale restaurant - reservations needed. **Prices** Cover ranges from £18-25, depending on the night's entertainment. Wine, beer, and mixed drinks start at £3. **Web Site** www.jazzcafe.co.uk **Dress** Smart casual. **Hot Nights/When to Go** Check the web site for show times.

Tip from Adam: "Check the web site to see who's playing. Many times it will be someone you've heard of or would want to see. Even though it can be pricey, this venue attracts some great names and is a cool place."

Mint Bar

Bar	18 Kentish Town Road	**Night**
Daily until 2am		

The Scene Small and dark with a cool, bluish-green glow, the Mint Bar is basically one big dance floor. In Camden Town, people come here earlier in the week, when other local bars are not open as late, but even then, it rarely gets crowded. This place prides itself on live bands and local DJs. The vibrant yet relaxing decor and superb sound system have a way of keeping you up on your feet. **Crowd** A typical Camden Town crowd - alternative and not as fashion conscious as in other parts of London. Locals and foreigners mix here with great regularity. **Entertainment/Music** Three live bands on Wednesdays; the second Friday of every month showcases local DJs. Every Monday is home to a night they call "The Mix". **Food/Misc** Upstairs balcony has the occasional private party. **Prices** Happy hour from 5pm-8pm with 2 for 1 on most drinks, cover charge can be £4 on Monday with beers for £2. Beers £3, jugs of cocktails £10, and selected shots £2; Prices rise on weekends and for special events. **Dress** Varies, so be safe with smart casual. **Hot Nights/When to Go** Happy hours for specials and Wednesday's jam.

Tip from Adam: "If you are in Camden Town, come here for the live music on Wednesday night. A very different scene from the touristy parts of London. A place you can chill out or get more into the music and hang out with laid back, chill folk."

The World's End	Pub/Café	74 Camden Street	**Night**
	Pub Hours (open until midnight F/Sa)		

👨 3	👩 4	👩 2	👩 4

The Scene One of London's most unique pubs…this place is absolutely massive, yet it maintains its unique character. There are two huge square bars, where you'll find almost any pint of beer you can dream of. The atmosphere is akin to being in the center of an old-fashioned town, because all of the walls are covered with windows of shops, the dentist office, a post office, etc. The ceilings are extremely high, and you can head up a spiral staircase to an upstairs loft with tables. Skylights let in the sun during the daytime hours, and a variety of huge flags fly from the ceiling's edge. This bar has an authentic feel and is a fantastic place to meet people or talk to friends. With all these young, friendly, and open-minded people, as well as these great beers and a really cool atmosphere, the World's End should be a must on your list of places to check out. **Crowd** Early 20s to late 40s. Folks here are laid-back and very friendly. **Entertainment/Music** A bunch of arcade/gambling machines, the music is sort of dark and very emotional…Coldplay, U2, Oasis, Cranberries, or some slow/retro techno. **Food/Misc** Traditional bar food w/ burgers, fries, chic sand, etc. for £4-8 (served only between 12-2:30 pm and 5-7:30pm). **Prices** Good selection of Beers £2-3, Wine £3-5 glasses and £10-14 bottles, Champagne £25 bottle. Mixed drinks for £3-5. **Dress** Casual - The location in Camden probably justifies the extremely casual, laid back, and even grungy style most people are sporting. **Hot Nights/ When to Go** Gets packed between 7-9pm, especially Thursday through Sunday.

Tip from Emma: "Come here during the week with some friends or on the weekend if you're flying solo. If you like Coldplay and bands with a similar style, you'll fall in love with the atmosphere here. The prices are reasonable, the conversation is thought-provoking, and everyone is friendly."

CHELSEA:

151

	Club	151 Kings Road	**Night**
	Daily until 3am		

👨 3	👩 3	👩 2	👩 2

The Scene Not a typical upscale London club, but whatever 151 lacks in lavish décor, it more than makes up for in atmosphere. Hence, patrons who have been coming here for years affectionately refer to it as 1 Dive 1. Although the sound system is barely audible, even when you stand right next to it, the energy on the dance floor doesn't suffer. The crowd here is fun-loving and quite inebriated, more so as the night goes on. In fact, THEY are the scene. Their excitement swells when a Bon Jovi or G&R song plays, and they carry on well into the night - no matter what music is playing. A fun, inexpensive alternative to the more sophisticated London nightclub scene, an especially good choice for a Thursday night. **Crowd** Many 20-30 year olds, and some guys from the English army. The women are friendly and not afraid to initiate conversation. **Entertainment/Music** DJ plays a wide variety of dance music. **Food/Misc** The only beer served here is Beck's. **Prices** Beer £4, mixed drinks £6. **Dress** Casual club attire. **Hot Nights/When to Go** Come around midnight and stay until close.

Tip from Tuck: "The girls here are great and seem fascinated by an American accent. That's a great segue to the dance floor, so don't hesitate to ask someone to dance."

606 Club

Club	90 Lots Road	Night
	M-W 7:30pm-late, Th-Su 8pm-late	

 2   3   3   1

The Scene With live performances every night, the 606 Club gets you right up close to the musicians playing some of the best jazz in London. The jazz is mellow and soothing, and with a bottle of wine and a three-course meal, you can splurge a little and overwhelm your senses. A candlelit basement right out of the 1920s makes this a great place to take a date (if you somehow get one while on vacation in Europe). **Crowd** An older crowd, but anyone can come out and enjoy a night of jazz. As one of the best jazz clubs in London, it attracts a crowd that knows its music. **Entertainment/Music** Live music every night of the week. The 606 Club gets some of the best jazz musicians in the area. **Food/Misc** Full menu. **Prices** If you are not eating here, they charge £7 to come listen to the music. Beers are £3.50-4, and they have some very affordable wines. **Web Site** www.606club.co.uk **Dress** Smart casual. **Hot Nights/When to Go** Take a look to see when they are getting the best talent, because they will be sure to highlight this on their website.

Tip from Adam: "If you like jazz, the 606 Club is sweet, because it gets the best in the area. It may be a little hard to find, so keep your wits about you until you get here!"

Boujis

Club	43 Thurloe Street	Night
	Open late	

 4   3   4   1

The Scene Arguably London's hottest club, Boujis is a home away from home for some of the most wealthy and beautiful people in the UK. It is a members club that allows non-members entry on slower nights or when the crowd begins to dissipate. You've got to look good to dance on this club's tiles and have some mega cash to feed your alcohol cravings here. Calling this joint posh is an understatement, so if you're not a high roller, you better at least look like one the night you decide to roll in here. The Hollywood-style entrance barely prepares you for the suave interior and spectacular intimacy of this club. **Crowd** Mid-20s to 50s…upscale, fashionable, trendy, wealthy people. **Entertainment/Music** Hip-hop, house, and techno…some of London's best DJs mix it up for this dance floor. **Prices** Expensive…£10-15 cover. Mixed drinks about £8-12, beers £4.50. **Web Site** www.boujis.com **Dress** Semi-formal, look good. **Hot Nights/When to Go** Try it during the week, if you're not a member.

Tip from Brittney: "If you want to bump into a celebrity or elbow up with some of the most successful people in the world over a drink, you've gotta check this place out. Save up for a few nights and then just blow it out here one time…be sure to have a few cocktails beforehand though."

Confidential Bar

Club	17a Harrington Rd.	**Night**
Open late		

3 2 2 3

The Scene This club has only been around for about 3 years but is on the rise. It's just around the corner from Boujis, so if you try to get in there and can't (don't feel bad), you can head over to Confidential Bar for a few hours. Drinks can be a little pricey, but they play great, old-school hip-hop. This place is small and intimate with a true, retro club feel, and the back has a great area to hang out, lounge around, and meet people. **Crowd** A young crowd that is looking for a good time in Chelsea but can't afford or get into the exclusive clubs.
Entertainment/Music The DJ here loves to play old-school hip-hop, so be ready to shake your rump like a rumpshaker. **Prices** Cover is £5, beers are £4, and mixed drinks are £4.50. **Web Site** www.confidential-bar.com **Dress** Semi-formal to smart casual. **Hot Nights/When to Go** On the weekends, when you are in the area.

Tip from Emma: "A great option when you can't spend the big cash. The music takes me back in time and is awesome to dance to!"

Eclipse

Lounge	111/113 Walton Street	**Night**
M-F 5:30pm-late, Sa-Su 2pm-late		

3 1 4 2

The Scene This beautiful bar attracts London's most hip clubbers. A bongo player jamming on top of the bar contributes to a most lively atmosphere. Eclipse is the place to pre-game before hitting the city's most fashionable clubs. Guests here seem ultra-cool as they lounge around smoking and sipping fruity cocktails. As the cocktails take their toll, the crowd grows more vivacious and revs up to party into the early morn. **Crowd** A young and ultra-hip crowd, very sophisticated and high class. **Entertainment/Music** The man playing the bongos on top of the bar. **Food/Misc** The best watermelon martini in town, and the famous crack baby shot. **Prices** Watermelon martini £9, crack baby shots £5. **Web Site** www.eclipse-ventures.com **Dress** Something fashionable, though if you get here early (and don't plan on clubbing later), they are easier on dress code. **Hot Nights/When to Go** Get here 7-9pm, before the clubs.

Tip from Brittney: "Come here before going out to hip clubs. Make sure you get a table with friends and order these two drinks…the watermelon martini and the crack baby shot. Don't be afraid to try any of their other delicious cocktails, too. Oh my, they are just so good."

| **Harrods** | Other | 87-135 Old Brompton Rd | |
| | M-Sa 10am-7pm | | Day |

👤 3 👤 3 👤 4 👤 4

LONDONCHELSEA

The Scene Take a second to imagine the nicest department store your mind can conjure. Then walk into Harrods and realize that your imagination is weak, because you could not possibly have conjured up something so lavish and extravagant. This enormous 4 story shopping Mecca carries literally everything and at the highest prices imaginable. Find a watch for £30,000 (and it only tells time.) The décor is based on amazing art of ancient Egypt. Harrods carries the latest fashions from top designers, attracting tourists who simply want to feel connected to the high-life. Everything you can imagine is available here, so there will be plenty to entertain any shopper. Guys, can't stand shopping? Don't worry, there is an electronics department you won't believe. **Crowd** Many tourists come here just because of the name. It really is a sight to be seen. The crowd seems to love the fact that there is no entry fee and that they do not even have to buy anything. **Food/Misc** There is a restaurant on every floor and a large food court with a bakery, coffee shop, and a candy store out of Willy Wonka. **Prices** There has to be something you can afford, just so you can walk out of the place and say you bought something from Harrods. **Web Site** www.harrods.com **Dress** No dress code. **Hot Nights/When to Go** Go on an afternoon when you have lots of time to dawdle. **Close By** Harrods has spots to get a drink on every floor. Below the men's department on the basement floor is the *Green Room*, a pub that looks like it belongs in the club house at the golf course. Beers here start at £3.45. *Mo's* diner is a replica of a 1950s American diner, which serves hamburgers. You can even get Harrods own brand of beer here for £4.75. Below the food court is a little wine bar with a sophisticated look. They serve tapas for £5.95 and all sorts of wine. On the third floor is *Café Punch*, which is a very civilized eatery. Take a break from shopping here with tea and crumpets.

Tip from Brittney: "The Mecca of department stores. You may only get to go to Harrod's one time in your life, so just put something on Daddy's visa. If he gets mad, start crying and tell him you will pay him back, knowing, of course, that you never will."

Hyde Park

	Park	
	Until sunset ... April through September	Day

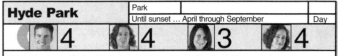

The Scene Get off the tube at the Hyde Park station, and you are literally right across the street from this amazing park. This place is big and beautiful, so be sure to wander around a little. As you enter from this corner, you'll find lush flower gardens to your left and a main path that leads you to Serpentine Lake, where you can rent boats, swim, fish, or just enjoy the view. **The Dell** is a great little snack shop on the corner of the lake where people pick up a beverage (serves alcohol) or a sandwich and chill out on the deck over the water. Continue past the Dell and see hundreds of Londoners catching some rays on the lawn to the right. You can rent a deck chair for a few pounds or just sprawl out on the grass. If you head across the bridge toward the other end of the lake, you can check out the swimming area and even public tennis courts, British bowling greens, putting greens, and an open field loaded with soccer enthusiasts. There is another snack shop/restaurant over here called the **Lido**, where you can catch more of a dinner after 4:00pm for £4-7. No matter what you do here, be sure to relax and enjoy yourself...everyone looks laid back and at peace. **Crowd** Everyone enjoys this park for one reason or another. You'll see plenty of hippies walking their dogs, as well as wealthy Londoners riding their horses around the dirt paths. Young and old alike, this park caters to everyone on a sunny morning or afternoon. **Entertainment/Music** Swimming, fishing, boating (all in designated areas), as well as horseback riding, bicycling, tennis, bowling, putting, and acres of open fields. **Food/Misc** The Dell and The Lido are two places to grab a bite. There are also plenty of hot dog and ice cream vendors scattered throughout the park. **Prices** The Dell and The Lido serve sandwiches, cold salads, some meats, and pastas for £3-6, cold drinks including beers for £2-3, wine starting at £12 a bottle. Different types of boats to rent for £4 per half hour and £6 per hour (children discounts and no credit cards accepted)... tennis, bowling, and putting are free, but bring your own equipment. **Dress** Whatever. **Hot Nights/When to Go** Open April through September.

Tip from Adam: "Forget your worries here people...hang out, eat, and drink on one of the lawns and then mingle with some of these chill folks; everyone is so friendly. If you feel the need, float out in a row boat to do some great thinking or just grab a dark beer at the Dell."

Maroush

Restaurant	38 Beauchamp Place	**Night**
Weekends until 4-5am, weekdays until 1am		Day

 4   4   2   3

The Scene The Maroush is the late night food choice for this neighborhood in London. The food is amazing and not very expensive. A seat at the bar will allow you to watch your delicious sandwich being made, or you can relax at a table. Both will allow you to enjoy the ongoing discussion of that night's "hot" spots, as late night revelers feast. **Crowd** Literally, people of all ages are here, but a twenties crowd of party-goers dominates the late night action. **Entertainment/Music** Lebanese Music. **Food/Misc** Amazing Lebanese food...the chicken/lamb shawarma is absolutely the best, very authentic. **Prices** £5 shawarma and other late night snacks. At dinnertime, you can sit down to a great meal for £10-20. **Web Site** www.maroush.com **Dress** Casual - anything goes. **Hot Nights/When to Go** Late night.

Tip from Tuck: "There is no better place to grub after a long night of pub and club hopping than Maroush. Come here late night for some unreal eats, and enjoy the energy of other young people on their last stop before home."

Raffles

Club	287 King's Road	**Night**
Daily until 3am		

3   0   4   0

The Scene Bring some energy and your wallet to this London club that has been around for over 40 years. The dim red lights create an exceptionally sexy atmosphere where well-dressed and good-looking people hit the dance floor with energy and style. The downstairs offers one large bar, a dance floor, and a lounge with exotic red couches. Head upstairs to find another bar and a smaller, more intimate feeling lounge. **Crowd** The clubbers at Raffles are in their mid-twenties up to their early-forties. A great club for singles or groups of people who aren't afraid to burn some cash and mingle with London's creme de la creme. **Entertainment/Music** You'll hear the latest and hippest R&B or hip-hop music all night long. **Price** £5 beers, £7.50 mixed drinks. Cover charge for non-members - £10...all night. **Dress** Gentlemen, don't be afraid to throw on your blazers, but in any formal club attire you will fit right in. **Hot Nights/When to Go** Head over on the late side...maybe midnight, after the pub scene is completely dead. Weekends are the most packed.

Tip from Brittney: "After bouncing back and forth between some boring pubs, you should get over to Raffles and get your groove on. This is definitely the "in" place, and I wouldn't miss its late night scene for anything."

"The Cod"	Pub/Café	17 Mossop Street	**Night**
The Admiral Codrington	Pub Hours		Day

LONDONCHELSEA

👨 3   👩 3   👩 1   👩 2

The Scene Depending on when you stop by, this somewhat refined pub may be quiet and laid-back with just a few groups of people catching up over drinks, or it may be packed with people dining and overflowing onto the great outdoor patio. You'll see a lot of suits and hear a lot of civilized talk around this place, but don't be intimidated; patrons aren't afraid to get rowdy and have some fun. An ever-changing mix of moods and people make it a neat spot to grab dinner.
Crowd Sloan Square is a trendy area, and The Cod, therefore, attracts an eclectic crowd ranging from mid-twenties to early-forties. You'll find many successful businessmen here for meals or just a pint. On the weekends, they turn up the music a little so even the early-twenties crowd, on their way out for the night, can be entertained.
Entertainment/Music Rock and British music playing lightly. Nice outdoor patio with tables. **Food/Misc** Great Eggs Benedict. Dining room with full dinner menu - lot of meat selections, extensive wine list. If Bloody Marys are your thing, you need to try one here…topnotch.
Prices £3 beers, dinners around £15 - 20, lunch about £10 , £4-6 mixed drinks. **Web Site** longshot@dial.pipex.com **Dress** Casual to Semi-formal for the dining room and on weekends. **Hot Nights/When to Go** Th-Sa around 7:30pm.

Tip from Brittney: "I like this classy, modern pub in a great area. Hit it for a nice meal and some drinks before heading around the corner to Eclipse, a great pre-club scene."

Vingt Quatre	Restaurant	325 Fullam Rd.	**Night**
	Open 24 hours		

👨 4   👩 3   👩 3   👩 1

The Scene How beautiful, a spot that never closes. Bustling with the hip post-club crowd, the atmosphere here is lively and loud. Folks are friendly and easy to meet, and portions are large, making this a perfect late night stop. We recommend the American breakfast, aptly named, as it is more food than anyone needs. **Crowd** The hip crowd that gathers here late night no longer cares who you are, so they are happy to chat you up. They may even clue you in to the after-party scene.
Food/Misc A full menu, but focus is breakfast food. No alcohol.
Prices The food here is a little pricey, but they can get away with it, because no one else is open. A £2 cover charge will mysteriously appear on your bill. **Dress** Whatever you wore out. **Hot Nights/When to Go** Go late night to eat after the bars and clubs have closed.

Tip from Tuck: "Bring your late night appetite to this place and order the American breakfast…pancakes and bacon stacked high with syrup on top. Sounds tough to take, but wait until late night hunger sets in."

HOLBORN:

Café Kick

Pub/Café	43 Exmouth	**Night**
M-Sa 11:30am-11pm, Su 12pm-11pm		Day

2   3   1   3

The Scene Right in a hip area of Exmouth market is a little slice of Iberian flavor. Café Kick exudes a Spanish and Portuguese vibe, creating a most jovial setting. The tables and chairs are old and don't match, which only adds to the authentic ambiance of this place. The little kitchen in the back is in plain view, so you can watch them prepare the tapas and get the feeling that they are preparing them especially for you. Naturally, soccer is a main attraction, and three foosball tables going at all times make it only a more unique experience. **Crowd** A mix of internationals frequent this venue… Londoners, Spaniards, Portuguese, and Italians. Everyone loves to come to play foosball and for the happy hour specials. **Entertainment/Music** They play all kinds of Latin music, especially Salsa. Three foosballs tables open up for use every day at 3pm. **Food/Misc** A great tapas menu and other Latin type dishes. **Prices** Happy hour every day from 4-7pm, £4 cocktails for which they are known; £1.50 beer. The happy hour beer changes every day. Food is reasonably priced. **Web Site** www.cafekick.co.uk **Dress** No dress code. **Hot Nights/When to Go** Happy hour 4-7pm

Tip from Emma: "At 6 o'clock on Fridays, Café Kick is a jumpin' place to enjoy cheap drinks, meet people from all over Europe, and play some foosball!"

The Fabric

Club	77a Charterhouse St	**Night**
Fr 10pm-5am, Sa 10pm-7am, Su 10pm-5am		

3   4   4   1

The Scene This is not a place for the faint of heart. If you're looking to experience the ultimate in hard-core late night partying, then you've found your place. Fabric is a monster of a nightclub loaded with ravers and serious party people. You'll hear everything from hip-hop to intense house beats in this castle-like cave of a club. It gets absolutely packed on the weekends, and even the stairwells are crammed with clubbers taking a break from the green lights and thunderous bass of the dance floor. There seem to be infinite rooms and bars in this club, including a VIP room upstairs with a great balcony view of the main dance floor. **Crowd** Lots of young, open-minded ravers. Early 20s to early 40s. **Entertainment/Music** Two large dance floors packed with ravers dancing to some of the best techno DJs around. The light show here is not to be missed. **Food/Misc** If you want to wash your hands, you have to step on a button to activate the sink. Otherwise, you look like a monkey. **Prices** Cover-£12-20. **Dress** Club Attire. **Hot Nights/When to Go** Fri/Sat after 12:30am.

Tip from Adam: "Make this a must on your late night weekend agenda. This place is unreal! The light-music combination hits you like a one-two punch. Bottom line, you won't see many places like this in your lifetime."

Ye Olde Chesire Cheese

Pub/Café	145 Fleet Street	**Night**
See Hours Below		Day

3 3 1 4

The Scene Rebuilt in 1667, after the Great Fire - yes, we did say rebuilt - Ye Olde Cheshire Cheese has actually been a pub or tavern since at least the 15th century. In a word, this place is historic. Old photographs of pub drinkers line the walls, and the narrow spiral staircases and hallways lead you to bar after bar after dining room - so many, in fact, that it's easy to get lost. On the weekends, the cellar is the place to hang out and meet the younger crowd that comes here for the best beer prices in London. On a nice day, the courtyard out front can get quite busy too and provide a pleasant place to throw a few back.
Crowd During the week, a lot of business people come here after work, because the pub is located in a business district. Starting on Thursdays, lots of American students come here from nearby King's college.
Entertainment/Music Music in the cellar only. **Food/Misc** Limited bar menu. **Prices** Sam Smith pint of bitter £1.68, and the lager is £1.95.
Dress No dress code. **Hot Nights/When to Go** Th & F around 6pm.
Hours M-F 11am-11pm, Sa 11am-3pm, 5:30pm-11pm, Su 12pm-3:30pm.

Tip from Emma: "The cheapest beers that I have found in London yet. The cellar bar on Thursdays and Fridays really gets going in early evening. Lots of American students congregate, and the atmosphere is very social."

KING'S CROSS

The Backpacker

Pub/Café	126 York Way	**Night**
F-Sa 8pm-2am, Su 4pm-12am		Day

4 3 3 4

The Scene The original party pub since 1991, The Backpacker provides a sweet time for all. Sawdust floors, rowdy (sometimes costumed) crowds, loud music, serious dancing, and a lively patio culminate in a unique party scene. This boisterous crowd makes its way here by bus after a Sunday afternoon of drinking at The Church. Although their costumes show the wear of the day, patrons have lost none of the verve with which they began. The bar and dance floor bump with a dance beat, and they party spills onto the patio. The atmosphere has an Australian vibe, which attracts many happy, stumbling party-goers. **Crowd** A young party crowd...even though the bar has an Australian vibe, the crowd is a mix of English, Americans, and Australians. **Entertainment/Music** DJs play a variety of dance music. **Food/Misc** All you can drink Friday and Saturday from 8-10pm for certain beers and liquors, a shot called Green Death (which is rumored to have been banned in most bars), and a shot chair for the wild ones. **Prices** Cover charge £3 on Sunday, beers start at £2.50, mixed drinks £2.50. **Dress** Anything goes, even costumes. **Hot Nights/When to Go** Sunday afternoon after the church, but if you miss *The Church*, The Backpacker cranks up around 4:30pm.

Tip from Tuck: "Follow the crowd from The Church here on Sunday. It's impossible not to have a good time. I recommend the shot chair if you are feeling a little wild. If not, grab a table on the patio and chill until the crowd moves on to The Walkabout."

Filthy McNasty's Whisky Café

Pub/Café	68 Amwell St	**Night**
	M-Su 12pm-11pm	

👨 2   👩 3   👩 1   👩 3

The Scene With a style quite its own, Filthy McNasty's is smaller, darker, and doesn't have the 'standard' rich wood paneling of typical English pubs. This is a real neighborhood bar where the entertainment is supplied both by the bar itself and its patrons. Known for its enormous choice of whiskeys, as well as the variety of clientele, there is a true, local neighborhood mystique and charm about this place. Filthy McNasty's is worth checking out to experience something a bit different from the standard pub scene, especially on Thursday nights, when there is typically live acoustic music in the back room. **Crowd** Mostly local, but Filthy's has earned quite a reputation and now attracts patrons from all over the city. A wide range of ages, from mid-20s to 40s. **Entertainment/Music** Every night, there's some kind of unique entertainment (from music to poetry and book readings). Thursday through Saturday, they offer live acoustic music. **Prices** Beers start at £2.50, shots for £2.50 or 5 shots for £10. Whiskey prices range from £2.50 and up and up. **Web Site** www.filthymacnastys.com **Dress** Completely casual. **Hot Nights/When to Go** Weekends for live music. Gets crowded around 5pm when the locals get off work.

Tip from Adam: "I love the laid back atmosphere of this neighborhood bar. It's a great place to sit back on a weekend and enjoy an acoustic performance."

The Walkabout

Bar	56 Upper St.	**Night**
	M-Sa until 2am, Su to 12am	

👨 3   👩 3   👩 1   👩 4

The Scene A sports bar with Australian flavor, the Walkabout has perhaps the best deals on drinks in London on a Wednesday night, which is student night. Students from the area pack this place to watch rugby, enjoy a cheap beer, or dance the night away at the back of the bar. Walls painted with references to Australian culture and Australian beer decorations hang from the ceiling. Who cares that you are in England; the crowd is fun, and the drinks are cheap. **Crowd** Mostly students congregate here on Wednesday nights, an equal mix of girls and guys. **Entertainment/Music** Dancing in the back with a DJ playing mostly techno type music or hip-hop remixes, Golden Tee 2005. **Food/Misc** A full menu is served here during the day and early evening. **Prices** Plenty of beers and alcohol to choose from for £1.50 on Wednesday; just ask a bartender which ones. £2 shots every night. **Web Site** www.walkabout.eu.com **Dress** Smart casual, though no strict dress code. **Hot Nights/When to Go** Wednesday all night, before 11pm no cover. Also, on Sunday evening, people come here after *The Church* and *The Backpacker*.

Tip from Emma: "On a Wednesday night, get here before 11pm to avoid the cover. Once in, there are plenty of drinks to choose from for £1.50, so be sure to take advantage."

Water Rats

Pub/Café	328 Grays Inn Rd	**Night**
Doors typically open at 7:30pm, but check website for schedule		

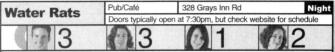

3 3 1 2

The Scene Water Rats is a run down looking café/pub/live music venue with a small stage that features three bands every night. The music styles vary greatly and can include heavy metal, rock, folk, and rhythm. The first band starts playing around 8:15pm and the headline around 9:45. If one of the bands doesn't fit your mood, there's a front bar area where you can hang and wait them out. **Crowd** Mostly alternative, but dependent on the bands playing that night. **Entertainment/Music** Three live bands every night. **Food/Misc** French fries, onion rings, etc. Bar snacks £2.50; A summer special all you can eat buffet £5.95. **Prices** Shots £2.30, cocktails £3.10. Cover ranges from £4-8. **Web Site** www.plumpromotions.co.uk **Dress** Casual **Hot Nights/When to Go** Check their web site for detailed info on the bands.

Tip from Adam: "Check the web site, because a lot of the bands here are hit or miss, but you'll definitely get your fix of live music. Also on their web site, you can download and print out a flyer that will get you a pound off the cover."

The Wenlock Arms

Pub/Café	26 Wenlock Rd	**Night**
Pub Hours		Day

3 3 1 4

The Scene Voted best pub in North London in 2004, the Wenlock Arms is the epitome of a traditional English Pub. While many other pubs in London try artificially to create that old feel, this pub just flat out has it. In fact, the bar itself is still the original mahogany wood from 1863. Old beer mugs and bottles line parts of the walls, and each has its own story. Although it is located a little off the beaten path and is somewhat hard to find, the effort will be worth it. **Crowd** A local crowd that is very amiable and just loves to chat you up about America, beer, and pubs. It is definitely an older crowd (40s and 50s), but they still like to have fun and take it easy over a good pint. It's fair to say that they take their beer seriously here. **Entertainment/Music** On Friday and Saturday nights, there's live Jazz music. There's also a little piano set up in the corner, as well as a dartboard. **Food/Misc** Known for their hot beef sandwiches; the food is very inexpensive, and the portions are huge. **Prices** Beef sandwiches cost £2, beer starts at £2.10. **Web Site** www.wenlockarms.co.uk **Hot Nights/When to Go** Late afternoons are great, but it really gets going when the music starts on weekend nights.

Tip from Emma: " I love the classic, almost historic feel of Wenlock Arms, and the cheap food and beer make it a can't miss. The people here are just waiting to chat, so take a seat at the bar and enjoy the ride. You are sure to learn a lot."

NOTTING HILL

Bed

Bar	310 Portobello Road	**Night**
Pub Hours		Day

👤 2   👤 4   👤 3   👤 3

The Scene Bed is a place you really have to see to believe. Walking in downstairs, you literally feel like you're in another world. Candles are assisted by just a few dim lights to break the dark, intimate feel of this loungy bar. The smell of incense adds to the ambiance, as you grab a seat on one of many, gigantic leather seats (beds) to order a drink. The "Bedroom", with its own small bar and additional tables and couches, is upstairs. This place is a sight during the day, but gets even better as the sun goes down and the candles burn through the dark hours. **Crowd** Trendy, random crowd of all ages (predominantly 20s and early 30s). **Entertainment/Music** Trendy, urban, modern techno with a slow, smooth feel. **Food/Misc** Small bar snacks. **Prices** Shooters £2.50; Cocktails £5-7; Bottled beer £2-3. Never a cover charge. **Web Site** www.styleinthecity.co.uk **Dress** Casual but trendy. **Hot Nights/When to Go** Sunday is a great afternoon/evening to check this place out.

Tip from Adam: "This, my friends, is a hot joint. Hit this place up after sunset and get groovy on one of the beds. This place just makes you feel good somehow, and the music, candles, incense combo leave you in a peaceful trance."

The Market Bar

Bar	240A Portobello Road	**Night**
Pub Hours		Day

👤 3   👤 2   👤 2   👤 3

The Scene A great bar/pub in which to hear some live jazz and mellow out a little. Although this large venue is covered in wood, it projects a very modern feel. It's got an urban style with high ceilings and tons of space. When the live music isn't playing, you can hear the friendly chatter from inside all the way on the street. Definitely stop in here for some socializing and a great cocktail. There are even a couple of TVs, if you need to check the score of a futbol or cricket match. **Crowd** Eclectic, young, stylish…early 20s to late 30s. Given the hip location, this is a place where you will actually see some preppy characters. **Entertainment/Music** Hip, groovy music, a lot of conversation here…it's loud inside from all the people talking. **Food/Misc** Live jazz every Sunday from 4-7pm and other live music on Fri/Sat. **Prices** Shooters £3.50, cocktails £4.50, glasses of wine £3-£4, Jugs of Pimm's lemonade & fruit £13.50. **Web Site** www.massivepub.com **Dress** Casual. **Hot Nights/When to Go** F/Sa or on Sunday afternoon if you like live jazz music. **Close By** Upstairs is the *Market Thai Restaurant*, which is very trendy and has a good reputation.

Tip from Emma: "The jugs of Pimm's & lemonade are loaded with fruit and are actually very reasonable if you split the bill with friends. Grab one of these and a table for a while if you need to rest from all of the window-shopping."

Mau Mau Bar

Bar	265 Portobello Road	**Night**
M-Sa 11am-11pm, Su 12pm-11:30pm		Day

👤 3 👤 4 👤 2 👤 3

LONDON / NOTTING HILL

The Scene As you head down Portobello Road from the tube stop, you'll find this place on the left. It's hard to miss though, because you can hear the live music from about 50 yards away, and it rocks! This is an amazing place to grab some drinks, get off your feet, and enjoy live music in the comfort of a tropical, Jamaican-style bar. Mau Mau has a smooth, authentic feel, so it's more true Jamaican than cheesy resort. If exotic cocktails are your thing, you'll be in a tropical heaven at Mau Mau. **Crowd** Very diverse, young at heart, and fun. The people may be of all ages, but they come together to relax in this "tropical" getaway bar. Everything is casual, and everyone is super-friendly. **Entertainment/Music** Reggae Tuesday; Jazz Thursday. Live music Friday and Saturday afternoons and all day Sunday. Random live music/DJs throughout the week. **Food/Misc** Small bar menu. **Prices** £3 beer pints (some are even less expensive), £6 cocktails/ mixed drinks, Coffee, Sodas £1-3. **Dress** Anything goes **Hot Nights/When to Go** Tuesday and Thursday-Sunday.

Tip from Adam: "Spend a Saturday afternoon cruising Portobello road doing some shopping and pop into Mau Mau for a beverage and some great live jams!"

Notting Hill Arts Club

Club	21 Notting Hill Gate	**Night**
M-Th 6pm-1am, F 6pm-2am, Sa 4pm-2am, Su 4:30pm-12:30am		

👤 2 👤 3 👤 3 👤 2

The Scene Head downstairs to this basement with funky shadows and crazy art covering the walls. This place brings out the artist in everyone. There is one circular bar in the middle and a stage to one side for the live bands. Funky, urban chairs and couches against the walls blend into this hotspot for liberal, open-minded Londoners. They put out a program every week, so check the website to read up on who is playing when. They take their music very seriously here and like to support hip, trendy, new artists. A fun, different experience in London **Crowd** Art lovers of all forms. Very hip, modern, and opinionated. **Entertainment/Music** Wednesday-Saturday live music in the afternoons, otherwise DJs. Music varies depending on the night. **Food/Misc** Bar snacks at best. **Prices** F-Sa free until 8pm, £6 before 11pm and £8 after. Su £5 after 6pm, and M-Th £5 after 8pm. Absinthe £4.50, beers £3.50, cocktails £5.50. Until 5pm Mondays-Saturdays and 7pm on Sundays, £4.50 cocktails and other reduced prices.
Web Site www.nottinghillartsclub.com **Dress** No suits and no team jerseys. **Hot Nights/When to Go** Depends on what type of music you like…check website.

Tip from Adam: "This place is filled with interesting people following their dreams in the worlds of art and music. The cover isn't too bad, the drinks are great, and this intimate lounge puts out a totally unique vibe. I recommend coming when live music of your favorite genre is playing, so check the web site."

Portobello Market

Outdoor activity	Notting Hill Tube
	Day

3 4 3 4

The Scene This is a great place to spend a Saturday morning or afternoon. Get off at the Notting Hill tube stop and just follow the crowd around the corner to Portobello road. This is an absolutely beautiful area of London. For the first 10 or 15 minutes of your walk, you'll pass through a series of antique and upscale boutiques. Be sure to make an effort to see the entire street though, because as you wander, you'll pass through stands with fresh fruits, vegetables, fish, and all kinds of other fresh and interesting foods. The streets are loaded with all kinds of people, and everyone is doing a little shopping, browsing, or taking photos of this awesome scene. You'll notice, as you continue down the road, that it starts to become more of a hippie scene with cool, new age, flea-market style "stuff" being pawned everywhere. From trendy clothes and jewelry to homemade bongs, the eclectic wares here make this a fun area to check out. Live music streams out of the bars, and a variety of people perform in the streets. You can't help but be entertained. For cool places to get off your feet, check out the bars in the Notting hill area...most of them are right on Portobello road, and they have a lot of character. **Crowd** Runs the gamut…young to old, hippies to families with small children. Different areas of the market typically attract their respective audiences. **Entertainment/Music** Live music in bars, street entertainers including a magic booth. **Food/Misc** Tons of restaurants lining both sides of the street. **Dress** Whatever you want. **Hot Nights/When to Go** Saturday afternoon; Small scale version on Sundays. **Close By** *Hummingbird Bakery*: If you need a cup of coffee or some fresh treats, pop in here (about 5 minutes down Portobello on your left). You can watch them baking goodies right in front of you. *Cafe Groove*: Further down Portobello Road on your left, Groove has a rooftop patio where you can check out the street scene from above while re-fueling with a cup of java.

Tip from Emma: "Talk about sensory overload, this place has it all! There's enough here to keep you entertained for hours, if not the whole day. Just make sure to give your self enough time here - you won't regret it!"

WEST END:

Alphabet | Bar | 61-63 Beak Street | **Night**
| | M-F 11am-11pm, Sa 4-11pm, Su Closed |

🧑 3   👩 4   👩 4   🧑 3

The Scene One of London's first urban bars, Alphabet maintains its funky and modern style to this day. With a map of its surrounding neighborhood painted on the floor in the basement, this place is as true to SoHo as SoHo is to it. The venue is comprised of a bar upstairs with plenty of tables and groovy chairs, as well as a bar downstairs with leather car seats to enjoy. Thursday through Saturday, DJs turn tables to create a funky, urban beat that represents this intimate bar perfectly. The management is friendly, and the atmosphere is super-cool without a pretentious feel. Be sure to check out the very comprehensive website, which uses every letter of the alphabet to describe this one-of-a-kind bar. **Crowd** Media, SoHo artists, young professionals, very liberal. Early-20s to mid-40s...this place attracts everyone with a heartbeat. **Entertainment/Music** Urban, Modern techno/house music... absolutely amazing tunes. **Food/Misc** Eclectic menu £2-9. First Wednesday of every month, there a big art exhibit features a different artist. **Prices** All premium alcohol...specialty mixed drinks £5-8, beers £3, shooters £3-4, bottles of house wine starting at £13.50.
Web Site www.alphabetbar.com **Dress** Smart Casual. **Hot Nights/When to Go** Popular all week long (lots of local SoHo regulars).

Tip from Brittney: "Everyone here is so stylish and cool...you feel like your gonna bump into David Bowie or some famous artist. My advice is to come here anytime, because it's always a party."

The Argyll Arms

Pub/Café	18 Argyll Street	**Night**
Pub Hours (open until midnight F/Sa).		

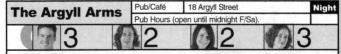

3 2 2 3

The Scene Exceptionally large and with a lot of character, this classic pub is covered in old-fashioned, antique, finished wood with patterned ceilings and rustic carpets. Upstairs, the Palladium bar and dining area is a great place to sit down to eat, preferably by the window with a great view of the street below and the outdoor tables. On the weekends, the outdoor area fills up with Londoners around 7:30pm (if the weather permits), and the streets are filled with friendly chatter and laughter. There are bars upstairs and downstairs, but the best place to meet people and mingle is downstairs in the back or outside. **Crowd** Early-twenties to late-thirties…lots of well-dressed people probably coming here straight from work. It has a preppy and wholesome feel, and you can meet a lot of well-rounded professionals. **Entertainment/Music** Quiet rock music makes this a great place for conversation; gambling machines are spread throughout the downstairs. **Food/Misc** An extensive bar menu with the usual fish n chips/burgers to some salmon, shrimp, and good steak meals (£5-9). **Prices** Beers start at £2.20, mixed drinks at £2.70…double up on a drink for £1 during happy hour (5pm-8pm). **Dress** Casual to Formal…you don't need to get dressed up to fit in. **Hot Nights/When to Go** Thursday-Saturday evening…No real happy hour specials, except you can "double up" on any mixed drink for £1 (double the alcohol).

Tip from Tuck: "Come here for a great pub-style meal, and then head to the outdoor tables to meet some attractive British businesswomen. Argyll street is also a cool little side street to do some people-watching if you're not feeling too social."

Bar Italia

Pub/Café	22 Frith Street	**Night**
Open 24hours		

2 2 1 4

The Scene If you aren't quite ready for the night to end, Bar Italia is a late night beacon offering a fun, casual spot to grab a bite to eat and a cup of coffee and to catch up with many other young party-goers as they wander towards home. Not your everyday coffee bar, this place has life, loud music, and sidewalk tables perfect for meeting people on a nice night. Although they do not serve alcohol, the reasonably priced menu, good coffee, friendly Italian servers, and late hours make it a catch. **Crowd** Bar Italia attracts an eclectic crowd, primarily young to mid-thirties, finishing up a long night of partying. **Entertainment/Music** Loud primarily dance music fosters a lively atmosphere. **Food/Misc** Finger foods, as well as larger meals like pizza. **Prices** £2.10 for coffee, food starts at £2.10. **Hot Nights/When to Go** After a night of partying.

Tip from Emma: "Make your way here when you've had enough of the bars. A cup of coffee, a little bite to eat on the sidewalk, and a friendly crowd can be a great way to end the night."

Bar On Anon	Club	The London Pavilion, Piccadilly Circus	Night
	Daily 10am-3am		

2 3 3 2

LONDON WEST END

The Scene Grab your cocktails from one of the eight bars inside On Anon and enjoy the spectacular view of Piccadilly Circus. This place has something for everyone, whether you want to dance on the club floor, grab a table with friends in the lounge, or head up to the loft and chill out solo. This place is truly a combination of everything the London night scene has to offer, and the crowd is as eclectic as can be. Whatever your style, age, or mood, you'll fit in here. **Crowd** Waitresses are friendly and beautiful in this multi-faceted party place. The club floor and lounge are packed with London's hip twenty-somethings, while the loft and study offer a more relaxed environment for the middle-aged. If you are not mingling with your type...just change floors.
Entertainment/Music Techno/hip-hop in the club and softer, trendy music elsewhere. **Food/Misc** Extensive bar menu £7-£16. Happy Hour 5:00-7:30pm daily. **Prices** £5.95 premium cocktails, £3-4 beers, and £3-5 glasses of wine. Wednesday £3, Thursday £5, and Friday/Saturday £10 cover charges after 10pm. (No Cover Sunday-Tuesday).
Web Site www.latenightlondon.co.uk, www.onanon.co.uk **Dress** Anything goes, as long as you look respectable. **Hot Nights/When to Go** This is a great place to sit down with a bottle of wine during Happy Hour or come by at midnight to enjoy the club atmosphere.

Tip from Adam: "I don't usually like clubs or intense bars, but On Anon gave me just enough of that scene without being overwhelming. Kick it in the lounge, but be sure to at least check out the entire joint…it's hotter than I anticipated."

Bar Rumba	Club	36 Shaftesbury Avenue	Night
	M-Th 9pm-3am, F 6pm-4am, Sa 10pm-6am, Su 8pm-1:30am		

2 3 3 2

The Scene The scene at Bar Rumba is ever changing, but the focus is always on the music. Dancing, therefore, is a sure (and crazy) thing. Depending on your mood and style, you have a couple of enticing choices as you descend the narrow staircase into this bumping basement club. Whether you end up on the large dance floor with loud DJ beats and a raucous crowd or in the lounging area in the back chilling out with friends, you'll appreciate Rumba's variety. This place is nothing if not eclectic, but timing is essential, so don't forget to check the website for the night's theme. **Crowd** Rumba's crowd is diverse and ever changing, as are the music and the atmosphere. This place has something to offer just about everyone. **Entertainment/Music** Known for its eclectic music ranging from deep jazz, to drum n' bass, hip-hop, Latin, tribal beats, house, dance classics, and more. **Food/Misc** Well-known DJs on occasion. **Prices** £3-5 covers during the week, and £6-12 weekends (check website for exact amount that evening). Pitcher of cocktails £15, shooters £3.60, beers £3.30, mixed drinks £3-5. Specials 6pm-9pm on random nights. **Web Site** www.barrumba.co.uk/ **Dress** Casual club wear. **Hot Nights/When to Go** F/Sat or whenever they are playing your favorite tunes.

Tip from Adam: "Use your student ID to pay a cheaper cover and chill on some of the couches while listening to funky beats. Let the deep jazz sooth your soul."

Blue Posts

Pub/Café	28 Rupert Street	**Night**
Pub Hours		

👤 2   👤 3   👤 0   👤 2

The Scene This is another, traditional British pub with one outstanding feature…its live, FREE stand up comedy Monday through Wednesday every week. The place has a quasi-antique feel with old, dusty books scattered around shelves on the walls and wood-finished tables and stools. There is a room upstairs with nothing but big, wooden tables (where the comedy is), which is great for large groups to take over. The scene here can be a little quiet, but it's really good with a group of people to sit down and not be bothered. Alternative rock seems to prevail on the sound system, but bartenders are given some freedom to select the music...so beware. **Crowd** The crowd seems to be predominantly tourists, but some locals frequent this place as well, especially on comedy nights. People of all ages pop in, but nobody tends to make a night out of this place. **Entertainment/Music** Bartenders can pick what CDs they play, so it really varies. **Food/Misc** Typical bar menu (basic) £4-7. **Prices** No cover…Beers about £3, wine £3-4 a glass. **Web Site** www.philklein.co.uk for the stand up comedy, not the pub **Dress** Completely casual **Hot Nights/When to Go** M-W at 8:15pm for free stand up comedy

Tip from Adam: "There's not much to do on Mondays anyway, so definitely check out the live stand up comedy at 8:15…it's free. Drinks are pretty cheap here, and the place is pretty chill, so you may want to hang out for a little while."

Boheme Kitchen and Bar

Restaurant	19 Old Compton Street	**Night**
M-Sa 11:00am-1:00am, Su 12:00pm-11:00pm		Day

👤 3   👤 3   👤 2   👤 2

The Scene This is a traditional and modern version of Café Boheme, without the late night scene. The Boheme Kitchen and Bar has a great menu, including Lobster dinners and a variety of seafood dishes. The loungy feel inside, with trendy tables and chairs surrounding an island bar in the middle, is inviting. You may even smell some incense or the plethora of candles inside after the dinner hours have passed. Definitely check it out for a great bite to eat or mingle at the outside tables with some eclectic SoHo locals. A very social place where patrons love to catch a fabulous late dinner and some drinks with friends. **Crowd** Trendy SoHo crowd, mid-20s to 40s. Though very eclectic, patrons here ooze style. **Entertainment/Music** Trendy yet sophisticated techno music, not too loud. **Food/Misc** Extensive menu including variety of seafood…lobster dinner for two for £35, prawns, etc. Meals are £10 -15 with starters for £ 4-7. **Prices** No cover charge…Beers £3-4, specialty cocktails £5-6, glasses of wine £3-5. **Web Site** www.bohemekitchen.co.uk **Dress** Smart Casual. **Hot Nights/When to Go** Dinner time and into the night.

Tip from Adam: "Come here for some amazing seafood and throw back some cocktails. The crowd is real groovy, and the feel of this place is modern and funky. As things quiet down here, just head next door to Café Boheme for some late night drinking…it's almost exactly the same."

Brewmaster

Pub/Café	37 Cranbourne St.	**Night**
Pub Hours		

2 3 1 3

The Scene A traditional pub with a modern attitude is how the Brewmaster bills itself, and rightly so. The upscale interior with a traditional English pub feel is enhanced by a comfortable upstairs lounge and great outdoor patio, perfect spots to sip a pint. Its friendly atmosphere and subdued energy, replete with hip-hop and R&B piped (somewhat quietly during the day and early evening) through the speakers, make Brewmaster a refuge from the craziness of Leicester Square and a good time in its own right. **Crowd** Locals and tourists mix here, as do the young and old. **Entertainment/Music** Hip-hop and R&B play somewhat quietly in the background until the energy swells later in the night. **Food/Misc** Traditional pub fare £3.75-6.50 **Prices** Beer £2.95. **Dress** Casual attire, no dress code. **Hot Nights/When to Go** Gets going around 9pm on the weekends.

Tip from Adam: "The area between Piccadilly Circus and Leicester Square on the weekends is worth checking out, but the clubs here are not for me. Brewmaster is…so stop in, grab a seat on a couch upstairs, and enjoy a pint in style."

Café Boheme

Lounge	13 Old Compton Street	**Night**
M-Sa 8am-3am, Su 8am-10:30pm		Day

2 3 3 2

The Scene The late night scene here is really quite incredible. In the heart of Soho, this trendy lounge transforms from a great restaurant to a hot-spot for funky party people. There is a lot of French flair inside this beautiful establishment, and some would liken it to a Brasserie. Patrons relax in a very upscale, bohemian atmosphere here without having to break the bank on a ridiculous cover charge. The tables outside are a great place to sit down and socialize during the afternoon. **Crowd** The crowd is stylish, young, and hip. Media people, students, and young professionals seem to flock to this café. Draws primarily a young-20s to mid-30s group (especially later in the night). **Entertainment/Music** Groovy house music, very trendy. **Food/Misc** Extensive menu (£12-16 entrées), seafood, steaks, etc. Starters are £4-7. **Prices** £4 cover after 11:00pm F/Sa. Beers £3-4, glasses of wine £3-5, spirits £3.75, £5-6 specialty cocktails. **Web Site** www.cafeboheme.co.uk **Dress** Smart Casual **Hot Nights/When to Go** After the pubs close, this place fills up, especially on the weekends with late night partiers.

Tip from Brittney: "I love the feel of this chic spot…the décor, the people…so much to see. It has an energy about it while still being relaxed. I can get into this late party scene."

Click	Club	84 Wardour St.	**Night**
	Open until 3:30am on the weekends, M-Th 3am		

3 1 2 1

The Scene The experience here on a Friday night is unlike any other London nightclub. The quick frisking by the bouncers might seem to suggest a rough crowd, but patrons here want simply to dance the night away to the latest Hip-hop. The tempo on this dance floor never slows, and the crowd grows friendlier as the night progresses. Plenty of couches when you tire of the frenetic pace on the floor or want some private time. Plenty of love displayed here. **Crowd** A young, culturally diverse, 20-something crowd. **Entertainment/Music** DJ plays exclusively hip-hop music. **Prices** Cover charge £15 on Fridays, shots £7, mixed drinks £6-9. **Dress** Dressy club attire. **Hot Nights/When to Go** Late-late-night, so head here after the other clubs close, if you still want to party.

Tip from Tuck: "Keep an open mind and you may have quite an unusual experience here. Stay on the dance floor for a real adventure late night - you never know what might happen here."

Covent Garden Piazza	Square	
		Day

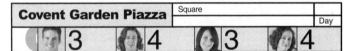

3 4 3 4

The Scene Free daytime entertainment and people-watching at its best... Covent Garden Piazza attracts all kinds and ages and is a fun spot to while away a nice day in London. Although there are plenty of shops, boutiques, cafes, and pubs to keep you busy or give you a spot to relax, crazy and obscure street performers are the highlight of the Piazza. Whether it's a man painted entirely silver, dressed like a leopard, wearing only a thong, or performing some feat like juggling knives while spinning a ball on a wooden spoon protruding from his mouth, there will be plenty to see and do. **Crowd** Attracts an interesting mix of tourists and locals, young and old, singles and families. **Entertainment/Music** Plenty of street performers and musicians. It is free, but performers appreciate a tip of at least £1. **Food/Misc** Inside and outside of the market are plenty of cafés and pubs. **Hot Nights/When to Go** Any afternoon. **Close By** The *Nags Head* - a traditional English pub, *Punch and Judy's*, *Vino bar*.

Tip from Emma: "Spend some time walking around and taking in all the sights and the free entertainment. I'm amused by the peculiar assortment of street performers."

Equinox

Club	5-7 Leicester Square	**Night**
Open until 3am		

 3   1   2   1

The Scene Offering all of the verve, flair, and beats of the more chic clubs (like the Hippodrome) without the outrageous prices, this scene is intense. A large but congested dance floor, flashing lights, heart-thumping music, and two incredibly beautiful dancers on their own mini-stages draw a passionate crowd to Equinox. The DJ spins (primarily hip-hop) above a dance floor that never slows down. Private nooks, however, provide an escape from the mayhem of the dance floor and a degree of intimacy. **Crowd** A young, international crowd reflecting the same lack of elegance and stuffiness as the club. **Entertainment/Music** DJ spinning hip-hop, beautiful dancers, advertised as a spot to watch soccer. **Prices** Cover £12, mixed drinks and beers £3.30. **Dress** Club attire. **Hot Nights/When to Go** Rocks all night on the weekends, but best to get here around midnight.

Tip from Tuck: "If you want that feeling of Hippodrome but can't afford the drink prices, come here. This is a lively dancing scene and a great place to meet women."

The French House

Bar	49 Dean Street	**Night**
M-Sa 12pm-11pm, Su 12pm-10:30pm		

 2   3   1   2

The Scene The French House is a very formal, sophisticated establishment. Beneath four French flags, gentlemen in suits gather here after work to discuss world affairs. The walls are covered in black and white theatrical pictures of the past. They open the windows so that people sipping a half-pint on the sidewalk can chat with folks sitting inside. A very civilized and cultured place to have some bar snacks (olives are free at the bar) with one of the many terrific glasses of wine they serve. Lots of history here, and, despite the tame crowd, it was once a wild spot that attracted some famous historical figures. **Crowd** Late 20s to old…a place of true class and dignity. **Entertainment/Music** No music…just intelligent conversation. **Food/Misc** Small typical bar menu (£4-12), pre-theatre menu 5:30-6:45pm (2 courses £10, 3 courses £12.50). **Prices** Only half pints of beer and an extensive wine list. £2-3 beers, £3-4 glasses of wine. **Dress** No dress code, but patrons are very well-dressed. **Hot Nights/When to Go** Before a theatre show or in the early evening for some food/wine.

Tip from Adam: "Come here, if only for an hour, to expand your thoughts and pick up some knowledge from this wise, aging Bohemian crowd. Don't waste your time with a half-pint…just enjoy some red wine and a few olives from the bar."

LONDON WEST END

Gardening Club

Club	6/7 The Piazza	**Night**
	Daily 5pm - 3am, Fr/Sa open until 4am, Su open until 2am	

LONDON WEST END

3   2   3   1

The Scene The Gardening club is very classy without being too "uppity". Located in the extremely fun neighborhood, Covent Garden, it draws a great mix of locals and tourists for happy hour cocktails or after dinner clubbing. There is a VIP room with its own bar for anyone with some charm or straight good looks (If you have neither, you can call ahead and reserve it). Dim red lighting sets the mood, and lounge style tables and couches surround a controlled dance floor. **Crowd** Mostly upper-twenties to late-thirties here. However, as the night progresses, the early-twenties appear to be the last ones standing. The friendly and laid back management contributes to a pleasant atmosphere.
Entertainment/Music Sunday 2pm live bands; Sunday night "Battle of the Bands" with £5 cover at 10pm. **Food/Misc** Mon-Sat, except Tuesday, Happy Hour 5pm-8pm (Reduced prices). **Prices** Monday £5 cover at 10pm (£3 for students). Tuesday £6 cover after 10pm. F/Sat £5 cover between 8 - 10pm or £12 after 10pm. Sunday £5 cover after 10 pm. Spirits start at £5, wines at £3.35, beer at £3.60, shooters at £2.50, and mini monte cristo cigars at £12. **Web Site** www.the-gardening-club.co.uk **Dress** Club attire. **Hot Nights/When to Go** Hit it on Tuesday for £6 cover and £1.50 drink specials (Happy Hour prices all night long.)

Tip from Tuck: "I like this place, because after hanging out in Covent Gardens on a calm Sunday afternoon, you can still party until 2am with a live band show. Come here on Sunday for the live music; there really is no better option."

The George

Pub/Café	183 Wardour Street	**Night**
Pub Hours		

3   2   2   3

The Scene Although this small pub attracts some tourists, it has an authentic, local feel. The quasi-antique décor, with futbol poster covered walls and three TVs airing sporting events, makes this a laid-back and comfortable spot to grab a beer and chill with friends. Only one bar, but plenty of tables at which to relax and enjoy a cigarette, a beer, and some conversation. Non-smokers, beware; this pub can smell like a chimney when it gets crowded. **Crowd** You'll find people of all ages here, but mainly mid-twenties to late-thirties. **Entertainment/Music** The somewhat subdued classic rock and hip music makes for easy conversation without shouting. **Prices** £1.65 bottles, £4-5 glasses of wine, £3-5 mixed drinks. **Dress** There is by no means a dress code and casual-wear blends you right in; however, like most London pubs, you'll see business attire as well. **Hot Nights/When to Go** Late afternoon… it closes at 11:00pm, so it will get crowded by 8-9pm on a weekend.

Tip from Emma: "This is a fun place to stop on the way to a club or even a bigger pub or bar. Have a couple of cheap beers and a cigarette before moving on to crazier places"

Hippodrome

Club	Hippodrome Corner in Leicester Square	**Night**
	M-F 9pm-3am, Sa 9pm-3:30am (closed Su)	

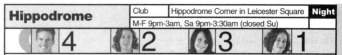

4 2 3 1

The Scene A London experience you must have to understand! Though not one of the city's more sophisticated venues, Hippodrome makes up for in energy and merriment what it lacks in class. The 500 plus young people thumping to Hip-hop on the enormous dance floor would agree that this is one of the biggest and best parties to hit on a Saturday. A massive dance club, brimming with beautiful (and somewhat provocatively dressed) people out to have a great time, may not be posh, but it's fun! Don't be surprised by the tight security with a metal detector and thorough frisking or by the random so-called magician wandering around in his tuxedo and top hat playing with a glass ball. **Crowd** A young (18-21 year old) and very attractive crowd comprised of locals and tourists from everywhere.
Entertainment/Music An almost exclusively a Hip-hop club with security tighter than an airport. **Prices** Cover charge £12 before 11:30pm, £15 after; £4 beers, £6 shots, £7.50 cocktails.
Web Site www.cirque@hippodrome.com **Dress** Nice club attire.
Hot Nights/When to Go Early Saturday (10pm) will usually allow you to get in without waiting in a long line.

Tip from Tuck: "A random, somewhat cheesy, and completely fun experience that you really should have while you're in London. This is just a happy place to be, and it doesn't hurt that the patrons are beautiful."

The Lab Bar

Bar	12 Old Compton Street	**Night**
	M-Sa 4pm-12am, Su 4-10:30pm	

3 2 3 2

The Scene There are 147 cocktails on this bar's menu, so bring your reading glasses. Lab, for the London Academy of Bartenders, is known for some of the tastiest, most well-made cocktails in the city. The scene is smart casual and relaxed. In fact, they'll make you loosen your tie and take off your jacket, if you're wearing one. Mellow music with a hint of African tribal beat complements the top-notch spirits and upscale interior of this bar perfectly. You'll meet plenty of young professionals, and during the week, bartenders from other London venues congregate for flashy drinks and bottle tossing. Check out the funky downstairs lounge with its own small bar and bathrooms labeled "Bastards" and "Bitches." **Crowd** Young professionals and the typical, open-minded hippies of SoHo who recognize a great cocktail when they taste one; Mid-20s to early 40s…anyone looking for great drinks and an intimate atmosphere. **Entertainment/Music** Mellow, smooth, trendy music with a hint of energy and techno. **Food/Misc** Small bar snacks for about £4-5…not much (people aren't here to eat). **Prices** No cover ever. Bottles of beer for a few pounds, cocktails start at about £6 and go up from there… shooters start at £5. **Web Site** www.lab-townhouse.com **Dress** Look good but comfortable. **Hot Nights/When to Go** This place is typically at full capacity (about 180 people) at 9pm on F/Sa nights.

Tip from Brittney: "Who cares if these drinks are a little pricey…they're some of the best fruity cocktails I've ever had! Come try this place out on the weekends before going to a club…it's especially great when you're with some people you know and can't stand to sip another beer."

The Langley

Pub/Café	5 Langley Street, Covent Garden	**Night**
	M-Sa 4:30pm-1am, Su 4pm-11:30pm	

3   2   3   3

The Scene At the Langley, you're really getting 2 bars and 1 restaurant under one roof. This place is quite extensive. Two very long bars with leather chairs and couches give it a funky, lounge feel. Low ceilings and dim lights shining on the yellow interior frame the funky house beats. This place screams retro and attracts trendy media-type crowd for dinner, drinks, or just intriguing conversation. The suave restaurant is in the rear, and you need to pass through two separate bars to get there...so grab a drink along the way. **Crowd** Young professionals and media, stylish folks from the Soho area, 20s and 30s. **Entertainment/Music** DJ spinning funky house techno W-Sa at 9pm, 500-person capacity. You can reserve funky rooms in the back with brick walls and trendy furniture for group affairs...call about 5-6 weeks in advance (doesn't cost anything unless you fail to show up, in which case they charge your credit card). **Food/Misc** An upscale bar menu including beef Wellington, sirloin steaks, fish n chips from £9-15, starters are about £5. M/Tu you get 50% off your food bill, and W/Th you get 25% off. You have to be 21 (not just 18) to enter. **Prices** Cover charge: £3 after 10pm on Thursday, £5 after 10pm on F/Sa. Beers £3, cocktails £5, glasses of wine £3-4. Happy hour 5-7pm for half-priced drinks. **Web Site** www.latenightlondon.co.uk **Dress** Smart Casual. **Hot Nights/When to Go** Thursday-Saturday for happy hour and after 9pm with the DJ.

Tip from Emma: "Come here for happy hour and enjoy 2 for 1 drink specials for two hours. There is no cover during happy hour, and if you stick around long enough, you'll hear great DJs pump some cool techno at 9pm."

The Long Island Iced Tea Shop

Club	1 Upper Saint Martin's Lane	**Night**
	M-Sa 12pm-3am, Su 7pm-10pm	

3   2   3   2

The Scene Long Island Iced Tea Shop is a surprisingly great club, even for those who don't do the "clubbing" thing. Dim blue lights set the tone in this two-story, trendy club, and the atmosphere is very open, more like a bar then a nightclub. When the downstairs club area gets too packed and intense, enjoy the upstairs lounge and smaller bar for a more intimate experience. The upbeat crowd seems to enjoy equally dancing to hip-hop/techno music and mellowing out on the couches. **Crowd** Everyone here is well-dressed but casual, proper without being formal. Patrons tend to be in their twenties or thirties and somewhat cliquey. This is a great place to come with a group. **Entertainment/Music** Hip-hop/Techno...loud. **Food/Misc** Burgers, Pizza, Nachos (£3-6) until 9pm. After 9pm, only a snack menu. **Prices** £5 cover charge on the weekends, lots of alcoholic iced tea drinks for around £5, great long islands iced teas and martinis for £5, shooters for £2.50, and beers for £2-3. **Dress** Casual club wear. **Hot Nights/When to Go** Come by late night on the weekends or for terrific Happy hour cocktails during the week.

Tip from Tuck: "This is my kind of club. I recommend coming by for a few very stiff, very good long islands late in the night and checking out the beautiful patrons."

Los Locos

Club	24-26 Russell Street	**Night**
M-Sa 5pm-3am		

👨 3 👩 3 👩 2 👩 3

The Scene This is a fun club without all of the red-tape and hassle. It's "crazy", as the name implies, with people bouncing to great music all night long. On one floor, a large bar serves decent cocktails at decent prices. This club has dim lights and some booth/tables around the dance floor, yet it isn't excessively trendy. It's a place for people who just want to drink, dance, and meet "normal" people looking to have some fun. **Crowd** Early 20s to late 30s…a great club to hit with a group of friends, but also easy to meet people. Seems like it fills up with middle-class, down to earth folks. **Entertainment/Music** Loud hip-hop and dance music, very new popular songs, DJ. **Food/Misc** Happy Hour 8pm-12am M, 5pm-late Tu, 5pm-12am W, 5pm-8pm Th-Sa - £1 beers, £2 mixed drinks, and half-price bottles of wine. **Prices** £5 -10 cover depending on the night, which is pretty reasonable given the fair drink prices and unpretentious atmosphere. £3 beers, £4-5 mixed drinks. **Web Site** www.los-locos.co.uk **Dress** Casual to dressy. **Hot Nights/When to Go** Either for happy hour or around 12am on the weekends.

Tip from Emma: "If you're going to splurge and pay £10 to go into a club, this is a great place to do it. I like it because it's not uppity, and people here are friendly. This is a great place to enjoy yourself, meet some people, and avoid chasing after "the scene.""

Mai Tai

Bar	39-45 Shaftesbury Ave	**Night**
Su-Th until 1am, F-Sa until 3am		

👨 2 👩 1 👩 3 👩 1

The Scene An upscale venue that manages to be fun as well, Mai Tai is about three things: lounging, dancing, and house DJs. DJ stages above the dance floor set the energetic tone for the young crowd with the latest dance music, while the upstairs balcony provides a break from the dance floor (and a great view of it) but not from the music. Plenty of private nooks offer yet another (more intimate) experience to share with friends new and old. A swanky night of cocktails and dancing to be had here. **Crowd** Attracts an eclectic crowd of 20-somethings. **Entertainment/Music** DJs play a range of dance music, house club style to hip-hop. **Prices** Cover charge £5, beers £3.30, mixed drinks starting at £3.30. **Web Site** www.maitai-london.com **Dress** Smart casual. **Hot Nights/When to Go** The manager recommends Sundays, as they are one of the few spots open late (1am).

Tip from Brittney: "The dance floors here are great, but I love sipping cocktails and relaxing on the comfy couches upstairs. Very posh."

Museum Tavern	Pub/Café	49 Great Russel Street	**Night**
	Pub Hours		

😀 2   👩 3   👩 0   👩 2

The Scene You'll feel as if you've stepped into a painting of a traditional, 18th century English pub with fine engraved wood walls and old Londoners conversing about art, literature, and politics - a painting you might see across the street at the British Museum of Art. The Museum Tavern epitomizes English charm with its ultra-classy décor and "conversational" atmosphere. With a range of unique draft beers and a glimpse into the city's history, this is a great place to meet London's older generation, who still enjoy a pint and conversation.
Crowd An older crowd, mainly in their 40s, 50s, even 60s, but the bartenders are young. Primarily a local crowd, but some tourist traffic attracted by the British Museum of Art. **Entertainment/Music** Light jazz or soft-rock piped in, quite soothing really. **Food/Misc** A full menu of sandwiches, and a house specialty of fish and chips for £6.95. **Prices** Beer £2.50-2.80, mixed drinks £3.10, food starts at £4.45 for a meal. **Dress** Casual, no dress code.

Tip from Adam: "After an intriguing cultural experience at the museum, relax at the Museum Tavern with the pint of your choice and chat up an old time local for a fun yet insightful experience."

N20	Bar	187 Wardour St. (Upstairs)	**Night**
	M-Th until 11pm, F/Sa until 1am, Su closed		

😀 1   👩 1   👩 3   👩 2

The Scene Young, chic, savvy Londoners converse here over beer and cocktails, seemingly enjoying the upscale décor and soothing atmosphere that N20 exudes. Modish furniture and chill techno beats create a look, sound, and feel that is modern and hip. Those who enjoy this venue as a great place to chill out before a night of clubbing will definitely know what's going on in town later. Although the bar/lounge feeling remains constant, live DJs spin low-key techno on weekend nights, and the crowd grows. **Crowd** A young, hip, under-30 crowd. **Entertainment/Music** Local DJ spins here on the weekends. **Food/Misc** Limited bar menu with calamari and salmon. **Prices** Wine £3, beers £3, cocktails £5, reduced prices M-Th until 8pm and all day on Friday and Saturday. **Dress** A little up from casual, but jeans and a nice t-shirt will not leave you feeling out of place. **Hot Nights/When to Go** Weekend nights, when a DJ is playing, are the best times to fully appreciate this bar.

Tip from Brittney: "If you are going to a club in the area, come here early to grab a quick bite. Then, relax with a cocktail to get into a 'techno mindset' before hitting the clubs."

The O' bar

Bar	83-85 Wardour	**Night**
Daily until 3am		

LONDON WEST END

4 3 3 3

The Scene The O'Bar is perfect for dancing, singing along with the music, or lounging, because you get a completely different feel depending on what floor you are on. The basement dance floor is open only from Thursday to Saturday. The small space gets a bit crazy, because the walls don't give you anywhere else to go, and you end up getting very close to the people all around you. The main floor has a modern and funky interior, which you may not even notice since the place gets so packed. The crowd here is not shy at all and loves to sing along to classic American tunes. To get away from the madness, the upstairs area is the place to chill. The upstairs rooms feels like it belongs in an old castle with soft music, a chandelier, and antique chairs and couches. A great place to party late night without having to be in a club. **Crowd** A young crowd (18-25) of Brits and Americans. People here are not too shy to get rowdy. **Entertainment/Music** Music is lots of classic American songs from Nirvana to Lynard Skinnard, and don't be surprised to hear "You've lost that Loving Feeling" on cue. **Food/Misc** A full menu is served all night, from small pizzas to sandwiches. Great to share late night eats. **Prices** Beers £3.20 and mixed drinks £5.90, food ranges from £3-8. Cover depends on the when you come and how crowded it is. Cheaper earlier in the night, but can get up to £10. Mon-Sat 5-8pm and all day Sunday £7 cocktail pitchers. **Dress** Smart casual, but not really strict. **Hot Nights/When to Go** Happy Hour 5-8pm M-Sa or come late (around 1am).

Tip from Tuck: "Even on a Wednesday night, this place gets packed. If you get here too late, you will have to wait in line, and no matter what you do...do not talk back to the bouncer. The line can be a great place to meet people before you head in."

O'Neils

Bar	33-37 Wardour St	**Night**
M-Tu 12pm-2am, W-Sa 12pm-3am, Su 12pm-12.30am		

3 4 1 2

The Scene A hot and sweaty bar with tons of people who really want to dance but want no part of London's clubbing scene. O'Neil's is a large, crowded, Irish pub, atypical in that its patrons party late into the night. The people here don't care how you are dressed or what you look like; they are happy to get to know you. Essentially, everyone here just wants to have a good time. With no true dance floor, dance wherever you find some space. **Crowd** An older crowd frequents O'Neil's, late 20s to 30s and even 40s. **Entertainment/Music** Loud music is always being played, apparently by a DJ somewhere. **Prices** £3.30 beers and mixed drinks, £4.50 double mixed drinks. **Dress** Casual attire, no dress code. **Hot Nights/When to Go** Arrive around 10pm before the crowds.

Tip from Adam: "This place fills up quickly, so come early if you want to actually have a place to hang out. O'Neil's is a great spot for me, because I love a loud and rowdy scene once in a while, but rarely want to go to a club."

Oxford Street Hostel

Accomodation	14-18 Noel Street	**Night**
		Day

👤 2 👤 3 👤 3 👤 2

The Scene A quaint little hostel that doesn't have the noise and commotion of larger spots, but is clean and has nice rooms and plenty of young people to meet. There is a great lounge with big and very comfy red couches and a television - a great area to meet other young travelers and kick back with a few drinks before going out. If you are looking for lots of party time, do not let the tranquility of the Oxford St. Hostel scare you away. It is in a great location, walking distance from all the sights, bars, and clubs in the West End. **Crowd** It generally draws a young crowd, but its cleanliness attracts even older people on a tight budget. **Food/Misc** There is a kitchen where you can prepare your own meals. They also offer a continental breakfast for £2.60, whenever you get up in the morning. They have internet (one computer), laundry (one washer and dryer), and they don't provide towels for free (£3.95 extra). **Prices** 2 bed room £24.60, 3 or 4 bed room £22.60, add £2 for all non-YHA Members. **Web Sit** www.yha.org.wk,www.yhalondon.org.uk **Close By** *The King's Arms* and *The Coach and Horses* are two traditional, social pubs right near the hostel that serve pub food (typical drink prices, etc). All of the bars of the West End are just a short walk from the Hostel.

Tip from Adam: "What I like about this place is that it is clean and quiet with a nice area I can lounge around in. It is in a great part of London, so I can walk out my door and have tons of fun."

Piccadilly Circus

Shopping	Oxford Circus down Regent Street	
Daytime		Day

👤 1 👤 1 👤 4 👤 4

The Scene Everyday, from Oxford Circus down Regent Street onto Piccadilly Circus, there are throngs of people doing what girls love to do best - shopping. This area offers a full spectrum of stores - from affordable (the Top Shop) to those that may break the bank (Adolfo Dominguez and Burberry). Liz Claiborne, The Gap, Talbot's, MGN, and Jaeger are a few of the many shops along the way. You really can get lost wandering around and spend hours going in and out of stores trying on clothes, shoes, or whatever. **Crowd** Mostly tourists of all ages walking up and down the street window-shopping and toting shopping bags. **Prices** A full spectrum of prices among these stores. **Dress** As you wish. **Close By** *Starbucks*, cool off with a fresh mango Frappuccino. *Cheers*, a tourist bar that gets the name from the sitcom; nice inside with a full restaurant. The back of this spot is designed to look like the bar on TV. *Jewel Bar Café*, Chandeliers hang from the ceiling, a smart casual dress code, very upscale bar/lounge, and lounge singers until 12:45 every night

Tip from Emma: "I love to check out all of the hot stores. London fashion definitely has a different feel from back in the States. The Top Shop on Oxford Circus has very affordable clothes and a 10% student discount."

Point 101

Lounge/Bar	101 New Oxford St	**Night**
M-Th 8am-2am, F 8am-2:30am, Su 8am-11:30pm		

2 1 3 2

LONDON WEST END

The Scene A lounge/bar with furniture that takes you back to the seventies - but not the real seventies. It's more like a futuristic vision of how people in the seventies thought the future would be - very Jetsons-esque. There are DJs every night that change up the genre from reggae, to techno, to hip-hop on the weekends. A very chill atmosphere with many areas to hang out and meet people over strong cocktails. **Crowd** A young, hip/alternative, and international crowd of Americans, Spaniards, Italians, and, of course, British. **Entertainment/ Music** Different DJs every night play jazz, funk, techno, or hip-hop. **Food/Misc** Limited snacks are served until 11pm. **Prices** £3 cover after 11pm on the weekends. Cocktails start at £6, wine £3.10, beers £3.20, mixed drinks £3.20, cocktail jugs only £12. **Dress** Smart casual. **Hot Nights/When to Go** Weekends - pre- night on the town.

Tip from Brittney: "This is a good place to hang out early and grab a couple of cocktails. A fun place, but better as a launching pad to get the night started."

Punch & Judy

Pub/Café	40 The Market	**Night**
Pub Hours		

4 3 2 3

The Scene The self-acclaimed world-famous Punch and Judy's boasts two bars in one, the cellar bar and the upstairs bar. Between the two and the fabulous outdoor space, this scene has appeal for every mood or personality. The atmosphere of the cellar bar is just as the name suggests, like a cozy basement. A fun crowd hangs out here after work - grabbing a bite to eat or drinking. On a nice day, the adjacent patio is packed with people having a pint and a good, relaxing time. Although the upstairs bar's décor is newer and more upscale, the patrons here are even more rowdy and drunken than those downstairs. The balcony on this level, which overlooks the square below, is the place to be in the late afternoon on a nice day. Packed with locals letting loose after a hard day's work and watching the street performers down below, Punch and Judy's is sure to be a great time. **Crowd** Primarily a mid-20s to 30s crowd. In the early evening, Punch and Judy's is frequented by young professionals, and the crowd gets a little younger as the night goes on. **Entertainment/Music** Small corner in which to play some video poker, but really just a drinking place **Food/Misc** A full bar/pub menu with very reasonably priced food. **Prices** Beer and mixed drinks around £2.90, food £5-15. **Dress** Many are dressed like they came from work, but no dress code - casual. **Hot Nights/When to Go** Late afternoon/early evening and especially during any big soccer event.

Tip from Tuck: " If you are in London on a nice day, make sure you go to the upstairs bar, grab a pint of Guinness, and find a spot on the balcony to be entertained by the street performers in the square below."

Roadhouse

Bar	35 the Piazza	Night
M 5:30pm-2:30am, Tu-Sa 5:30pm-3am, last Su of month from 2pm-1am		

4 3 3 2

The Scene This is a place meant to soothe the American soul for an evening. Heading downstairs, you may feel like you're walking into a classy truckstop with a mack truck coming through one of the walls, a Harley Davidson on the bar, and all sorts of road signs and decorative paraphernalia scattered throughout. The music is familiar and vibrant. Be sure to check the website to see who is playing, because this joint has live, classic American music playing almost every night. The dance floor is shaking, and there are tons of diner-style booths for those who want to relax and just let the music sink in. **Crowd** The crowd here is 20s and 30s for the most part. A good place to meet some fellow Americans amongst other Europeans. **Entertainment/Music** Live music almost all the time…check their website, but usually American classics from the 50s all the way through today. Some gambling and arcade machines near the entrance. Very loud place but a lot of fun. **Food/Misc** Typical bar menu: fajitas, burger, sandwiches £4-11. Happy Hour: reduced prices from 5:30-8:30pm. **Prices** Cover charge: Monday-Wednesday £5 after 9pm, Thursday £7 after 9pm, Friday £10 after 9pm, Saturday £7 from 7:30-9pm, £10 after 9pm. Beers £3-4, spirits £3, specialty cocktails £5-6, glass of wine from £3.50. **Web Site** www.roadhouse.co.uk **Dress** Smart casual… only clean sneakers, no futbol jerseys, no ripped jeans. **Hot Nights/When to Go** Saturday, this place is jam packed with people all night.

Tip from Tuck: "Get here around 8pm to catch the tail end of happy hour and to dodge the cover charge. This place plays awesome American music, and there are tons of Americans here to meet."

Ronnie Scott's

Jazz Club	47 Frith Street	Night
M-Sa 8:30pm-3am, Su 7:30pm-11pm		

2 4 1 1

The Scene London's oldest jazz venue is a members and non-members club, so it fills up with regulars, especially on the weekends. These patrons take their jazz very seriously, as well they should; legends like Jimi Hendrix have performed on this stage. Dim lights, comfy chairs and couches, and authentic "jazzy" decor set the mood for this one-of-a-kind spot. The cocktails are almost as good as the performers and the intimacy here, and it's fun just to watch jazz-lovers slip into a trance when the music starts. **Crowd** This crowd is a little older, maybe 30s to 50s, and very civilized. You'll fit right in with a nice suit and a smile on your face. Students pay only a £10 cover Monday through Wednesday, so the crowd will be a little younger these nights. **Entertainment/Music** London's most reputable Jazz Club, hence great Jazz. **Food/Misc** Snacks to meals. **Prices** M-Th £15 cover, F/Sa £25, Sun £8-12, students £10 cover M-W. Food £5-25, Spirits £7-8, beers £3-6. **Web Site** www.ronniescotts.co.uk **Dress** Dressy. **Hot Nights/When to Go** F/Sa, the main act usually starts around 11pm, but to get your money's worth, be here by 9pm to catch the opener.

Tip from Adam: "It's really quite simple here…if you love Jazz and can afford the expensive cover, you've got to check out this amazing club. Get ready to be blown away by some of these most famous performers."

The Social	Pub/Café	5 Little Portland	**Night**
	M-Sa 12pm-11pm		

| 2 | 2 | 3 | 2 |

The Scene The Social's decor and atmosphere provide some contrast to a typical bar scene. A narrow upstairs bar gives the impression that you are in a cozy cabin or a tiny ski lodge. With minimal space, it does not take much to assemble a good crowd, and people here get to know each other very easily. Downstairs is a bar and seating area just as narrow but without the warm ski lodge feel, because everything is concrete. With new DJs nightly, music is a large attraction here . A great place to take a break from the busy main streets of Soho.
Crowd Patrons range from 20s to mid-30s, with many media or aspiring media-types among them. **Entertainment/Music** Different DJs play here every single night of the week, so the music really varies. Social also has the Heavenly Juke Box, the best jukebox in London.
Food/Misc Claims to have the finest homemade pies in London.
Prices Wine starts at £2.60 a glass, beers at £2.90, martinis at £5.10, and snacks start at £3. **Web Site** www.thesocial.co.uk **Dress** To fit in with the crowd, you need to wear something hip or trendy; if not, go with smart casual. **Hot Nights/When to Go** Friday afternoon around 6pm is best. Generally more crowded during the winter.

Tip from Brittney: "A great way to spend time at The Social is to sit upstairs with friends in the u-shaped leather benches. You can hang out and take in the cozy vibe while listening to the Heavenly Juke Box."

Sugar Sugar	Lounge	187 Wardour Street (Basement)	**Night**
	M-Sa 5pm-12:30am, closed Su		

| 2 | 0 | 3 | 1 |

The Scene Sugar Sugar compiles numerous hip and modern touches to create a lounge as classy and alluring as they get. The atmosphere in this new London lounge is, simply put, smooth. Bold techno beats set the tone as you descend into this haven of plush, red couches and other furniture that looks like it is straight out of an art gallery. For the ultra-chic or famed crowd, private rooms are a huge draw. These require a booking and, at a minimum, a 45 £ bottle of Champagne.
Crowd The crowd here is young, beautiful, and fashionable, and there is an occasional appearance of a footballer. **Entertainment/Music** A DJ spins house beats. **Food/Misc** The private rooms here are the big attraction. On the weekends, there are 10 rooms with a 10 person minimum, and 2 rooms with a six person minimum. They require a booking in advance and a bottle of champagne. Food: chicken and burger platters for two for £11. **Prices** £6-8 specialty cocktails, £4 glass of wine, £3-4 beer. **Dress** Dressy club attire. **Hot Nights/When to Go** Friday or Saturday around 10pm.

Tip from Brittney: "If you can gather a large crowd, it's worth booking a private room for the night and enjoying some Champagne. If not, try to meet someone who will invite you in. The décor and atmosphere here are incredible."

Tiger Tiger

	Club	29 The Haymarket	**Night**
	Daily until 3am		

👨 3 👩 2 👩 4 👩 2

The Scene This huge bar/club/lounge attracts all kinds and packs them wall to wall. With four floors, each offering a unique party experience, it's hard not to find a scene that fits your mood. The upscale bar and dance floor attract the largest crowds and exude energy. Above, a more intimate dance area is lit with mellowing green light - a stark contrast to the loud beats and wild dancing by the bar. The adjacent lounge provides a great spot for groups to hang out and watch the action on the dance floor. The bottom floor discotheque has more dance space and louder music and is complete with red and yellow flashing lights illuminating crowds of people dancing by themselves. When the chaos that is Tiger Tiger becomes too much, seek refuge in the mellow, couch-filled lounge. Wander floor to floor or pick one and stay, you can't miss the vibrant scenes that set Tiger Tiger apart as a truly unique social experience. **Crowd** Attracts young people, tourists, and locals alike. Many here are beautiful and somewhat sophisticated looking. **Entertainment/Music** Primarily hip-hop here, but depends on the floor. **Prices** £10 cover on weekends, beer £3.30, mixed drinks £4. **Web Site** www.tigertiger.co.uk **Dress** You should be well-dressed in club attire not to feel out of place. **Hot Nights/When to Go** Gets crowded early and stays that way, but an earlier arrival will help you avoid a line.

Tip from Brittney: "I love the lounges here and, strangely, found that the best place to dance is by the bar on the upper/green floor. You won't feel out of place here."

Trocadero Center

	Outdoor activity		
	Daytime		Day

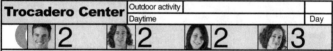

The Scene Located in Piccaidilly Circus, this large, very modern, almost futuristic looking shopping and entertainment complex attracts hundreds of tourists daily. It simply has something for everyone to do. Whether it's shopping or movies, ten pin bowling, arcades, or upscale lounges, bars, and clubs, the Trocadero center can awaken the child in you or appease your more sophisticated side. Your senses will be stirred by the sights, sounds, smells, and people that come together to make Trocadero Center the attraction that it is. The shopping here is decent, comprised mainly of "mall stores", but HMV Records has become a hang out of sorts - a great place to listen to music and sample video games from any system. **Crowd** A tourist destination, so the crowd includes tourists of all sorts. Many teenagers and families are attracted by the variety and economy - lots to do, cheap.
Entertainment/Music Ten pin bowling, movie theater, huge arcade, shopping. **Food/Misc** There are cafés and restaurants catered to grabbing a quick bite and sitting down to dine. **Prices** Bowling £4, arcade games £1, movies £5.50 for students and £7 for adults. **Dress** Casual. **Hot Nights/When to Go** Daytime.

Tip from Emma: "Go to the HMV records, listen to music, play a little Playstation 2 for free, then go bowling, so you can tell people you bowled in London. You can spend the day here without spending very much at all or you can splurge a little…whatever the case, you'll have a good time."

Waxy O'Connors

Pub/Café	14-16 Rupert St	**Night**
M-Sa 12pm-11pm, Su 12pm-10:30pm		

👨 3   👩 3   👩 1   👩 2

The Scene Many pubs in London try to create that authentic 17th-century pub feel; some are successful. And Waxy O'Connors... they try to make you feel like you are in the middle ages. Metal chandeliers, a medieval castle facade, a tower looking out over one of the bars, and a dark creepy forest bring a past era to life! The crowd and atmosphere are always lively. This is a great place to come in the early evening and stay until closing. Good music in the background at a volume which allows you to talk and to meet people. **Crowd** A young, non-clubby crowd that just wants to kick back with a few pints. **Entertainment/Music** Every Monday and Tuesday night, they have live music from 9-11pm. When there's no live music, they play classic rock, but it's in the background, which can be good. **Food/Misc** They have a full menu, typical of many London pubs. **Prices** Beers start at £2.95, mixed drinks £3.75. **Web Site** www.waxyoconnors.co.uk **Dress** Whatever you want, even sandals. **Hot Nights/When to Go** Friday afternoon, but it even gets good on Sunday night sometimes

Tip from Tuck: "If you are looking for one of the most fun pubs in Piccadilly, you should definitely not miss this place. Any day of the week it can be good, but it's best to come here on a Friday afternoon when folks finish working. Easy to meet people and lots of fun."

Zoo Bar

Club	13-17 Bear St.	**Night**
Daily until 3am		

👨 4   👩 2   👩 3   👩 3

The Scene Simply put, hit this new London hot spot any night of the week, and you won't be disappointed. Two floors are alive with young people living out Zoo Bar's motto: "Party hard or go home." The dance floors jump with hip-hop, techno, and remixes, as colored lights flash, creating a vibrant party scene replete with beautiful women. Energy abounds here! **Crowd** A young crowd - college age to mid-20s **Entertainment/Music** Dance here - mostly techno or hip-hop remixes. **Prices** Up to £10 cover on weekends, beer and mixed drinks £3.30, jugs of cocktails (3-4 drinks) £11.50, drink specials every day before 7pm: cocktails £2.50, jugs £6.95, shooters £2.50, bottle of wine £6, all champagne reduced by £10. **Web Site** www.zoobar.co.uk **Dress** Nice club attire fits well here. **Hot Nights/When to Go** Arrive between 10-11pm; it fills up quickly.

Tip from Tuck: "Get here early (around 10 pm), because this place fills up fast. Make sure to check out both floors. Girls are easy to talk to, so enjoy some conversation and dancing. With groups of friends, a jug of cocktails is the best bargain."

OTHER

Cantina del Ponte

Restaurant	36c Shad Thames	Night
Daily 12pm-11pm		Day

2	3	3	3

The Scene A large, open-air Italian restaurant with one of the best views in London, which makes a visit here well worth it. Located right on the Thames river, Cantina del Ponte offers a view not only of the water but also of the breath taking London Bridge. On a nice afternoon, the gentle breeze from the Thames cools you perfectly, as you relax over a bottle of wine and a nice pasta. A lively atmosphere and a great place to come with a large group of people. **Crowd** An older professional crowd frequents this restaurant, so it gets busy during lunch breaks and, of course, for dinner also. **Food/Misc** A full Italian menu with pastas, chicken, and beef dishes with sauce. **Prices** Bottles of wine start at £14.95, beers start at £3.25, cocktails from £5.50 to 6.95, glasses of wine at £3.95. The food prices are very reasonable… meals start around £6; Lunch specials from 12-3pm. **Dress** No dress code, but wear smart casual to fit in. **Hot Nights/When to Go** Any time during the week or weekend, especially on a nice day.

Tip from Brittney: "The best time to come here is on a nice sunny day. Sit out on the patio, order a glass of wine, and take in a great view."

Cricket

Sports	St John's Wood Rd.	
During the day, when there is a match		Day

3	3	1	2

The Scene Not too many Americans know what is going on when they watch cricket. It looks something like baseball, but the rules are very different. Nonetheless, a great day can be spent at the cricket ground, especially when there is a big international match being played. Just like an afternoon in the Wrigley Field bleachers (well, kind of), people have their shirts off tanning ultra-white bodies and drinking pint after pint. And if the sun isn't shining, people are just drinking pint after pint. Make sure to sit down next to a local so he or she can explain what is going on. It is not too hard to figure out, and once you do, the sport can be great to watch. **Crowd** A local crowd to root on England. People of all ages can enjoy cricket, though this is mostly an older crowd. **Entertainment/Music** Some of the finest Cricket in the world - we assume! **Web Site** www.lordscricket.com **Dress** Sunning attire. **Hot Nights/When to Go** Check the web for the schedule.

Tip from Tuck: "The best scenario would be to get tickets on the last day of an International test match. Sit back on a nice day and have some beers while learning a new sport and getting to meet local people. Just make sure to cheer for England, unless they are playing the US, but I don't think we even have a team."

Cubana

Restaurant	48 Lower Marsh	Night
	M-Th 12pm-12am, F 12pm-1am, Sa 6pm-1am	Day

 3   4   2   3

The Scene A trip to Cubana transports you from a bustling city to a bar on the beach in Cuba. With weathered rustic furniture in pink, green, blue, and yellow and plentiful Cuban references among the décor, the ambiance is decidedly Latin. Fake parokeets, Cuban flags, machine guns, and salsa dancers reinforce the motif, as does the festive salsa dancing. From Wednesday to Saturday, live Salsa dancing takes over, and patrons try their best at this sexy Latin dance. **Crowd** A lively and eclectic crowd comes from all parts of London - from government officials who live in the area to Latinos who come for a taste of home. Friendly patrons aren't afraid to try new dances.
Entertainment/Music Live Salsa Dancing form Wednesday to Saturday; any other time, they play Latin and Salsa-type music.
Food/Misc Cubana specializes in…Cuban food, so come here for the empanadas or any other authentic Latin dish. Happy hour 5-6:30pm, and Monday-Tuesday 10-12. **Prices** Cover charge £5 on Friday and Saturday. Lunch special: 2 courses £5.95, 3 courses £7.95. Tapas start at £5.95. **Web Site** www.cubana.co.uk **Dress** Super-casual.
Hot Nights/When to Go Happy Hour 5-6:30pm and for live dancing.

Tip from Emma: "Come here for happy hour specials and get a cocktail jug while sitting out front in the open air. You can make a whole night of it, so be sure to stay for the live Salsa dancing."

The Generator
Hostel

Accomodation	37 Tavistock Place	Night
	24 hours	Day

 3   4   2   4

The Scene This huge, full-service youth hostel offers anything you could possibly want from your accommodation, including a friendly staff available 24 hours and freedom from annoying curfews and restrictions. Most significantly, you don't even have to go out to find a party. London's Generator has earned its billing as a party hostel by maintaining its own lively, friendly, and rowdy bar with a retro feel, pool tables, and different themes and contests nightly with chances to win free drinks or prizes. The bar is open until 2am, and by that time, the crowd can become wild and super-friendly. Although life inside the hostel is pretty great, this place offers every opportunity to stay in touch with the world outside: there is internet service, plenty of telephones, an electronic touch screen enabling you to book hostels in other European cities, and a travel information booth. Its rates are hard to beat for rooms in London, and there are enough services that, theoretically, you could never leave the hostel and still have a great time.**Crowd** Attracts all sorts of backpackers and travelers from around the world. It attracts many younger travelers, from 18 to 25, as well as a strong hippie contingency. **Entertainment/Music** Bar/Juke Box/multiple pool tables/TVs/internet access/vending machines. **Food/Misc** Free breakfast daily from 6am-11am and inexpensive dinner options.
Prices £17 for 4 bed room/£16 for 5-6 bed room/£15 for 8-10 bed room. **Web Site** www.the-generator.co.uk **Hot Nights/When to Go** On the weekends the bar is packed by early evening.

Tip from Emma: "This place is as cheap as it gets in London for of safe, clean accommodations. Its also a blast though, so definitely book a room here if you're on a budget…they even have weekly rates."

London Pub Crawl

	Other	The Circle Line	
	Daily 11am-11pm		Day

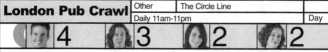 4   3   2   2

The Scene This rite of passage in London takes advantage of the variety, accessibility, and energy of London's social scene. Although it is often reserved for graduations, bachelor parties, or other ceremonious occasions, it is worth your while to try the crawl while you're here. Simply go to the nearest Yellow Line tube stop (notice the bottle shaped path that the tube takes around central London) and buy a pass for the day. Take the tube to the next stop, go to the nearest pub, and drink a pint. Get back on the tube and repeat. Proceed like this until you have made it around the entire loop of the Yellow Line (about 26 stops)…a crazy way to spend a day and night in the city. **Crowd** You and your buddies and/or traveling companions. **Entertainment/Music** A few stops into this crawl, you and your friends will be your own entertainment. **Prices** Beers average £2.50-3 at most pubs. **Dress** No dress code. **Hot Nights/When to Go** Whenever you have a totally free day

Tip from Tuck: "Don't make your first drink a Guinness, rather start with something light and then move on to the heavier beers. This might enable you to make it all the way around."

Open-Air Theatre

	Culture	Inner Circle, Regents Park	**Night**
	See Hours Below		Day

  3   3   3   3

The Scene An amazing way to see a show while in London. A very peaceful, earthy atmosphere with big green trees overhanging the venue, the Open Air Theater is a place to relax with a nice bottle of wine and experience some London culture. The lawn here is the perfect place to hang out with a group of travelers you know or want to get to know, not to mention the top-notch performances. **Crowd** Young and older people, lots of families. **Entertainment/Music** Check the web site for the current production. **Food/Misc** Buffet and BBQ, a range of home-made dishes, salads, and desserts. **Prices** In addition to having one of the longest theater bars in London, fully stocked with beers, Pimms, wine, and champagne, they also have a BYOB policy. Drinks start around £3. Ticket prices range from £10 to £28. **Web Site** www.openairtheater.org **Dress** Casual. **Hot Nights/When to Go** Check the web site for show times. Keep an eye out for the occasional late night performance. **Hours** M-Sa 8pm show; Th and Sa 2:30pm matinee, in season from end of May to the second week of Sept. Bar open until midnight.

Tip from Emma: "Buy the least expensive ticket, bring your own little picnic with a bottle of wine, and sit out on the lawn well before the show starts."

Regent's Park	Park		
	Daytime		Day

4　4　3　3

The Scene With its beautiful gardens and large pond bustling with ducks and rowboats, this park is truly a sight to see. But it isn't just the typical, calm, and peaceful park. Upon entering, you'll see the hundreds of people playing pickup soccer games all over the vast fields. In addition, there's cricket, net ball, tennis, or whatever you can imagine. While the sports are seemingly everywhere, there are still plenty of areas of the park that allow you to carve out a little niche and get away. Couples sit along the banks of the pond with a bottle of wine, as children play with the animals. Sitting in the gardens or along the pond is truly relaxing. It's a place so peaceful and serene, you'll want to whisper instead of talk. The ultimate place to hang out and marinate on a warm afternoon in London. **Crowd** All ages, sizes, and shapes. **Entertainment/Music** A tennis center with about 10 courts that you can rent for £9 per hour. Open-air theater with plays all summer. **Prices** Admission to the park is free. **Hot Nights/When to Go** Late afternoon on a sunny day. **Close By** Inside is *Queen Mary's Garden*: A little open air café that serves food for around £6-7 and drinks for £3-3.50. The *London Zoo* is open until 5pm and has an admission charge (and monkeys).

Tip from Tuck: "Come here in the late afternoon around 5 or 6pm and jump in a pick up soccer game. Everyone on the field is good, and the competition is fierce, but it is a great way to get some exercise and experience a different side of London."

Vinopolis	Museum	1 Bank End	
	M, F, Sa 11am-9pm, Tu-Th and Su 12am-6pm		Day

 4   3   4   3

The Scene An interactive museum for adults, Vinopolis is an amazing experience that gives you a virtual tour of wines from all over the world - starting in ancient Georgia, where wine is believed to be invented, to other regions of Europe, and finally to regions of the 'New World', including the Americas, Australia, and New Zealand. Set up throughout the tour are stations where visitors can taste wine and learn about each. As you make your way through the audio guided tour, the scenery changes to create the feeling of the location and time period about which you are learning. You'll even take a virtual tour of Tuscany on an Italian scooter! However, wine is not the only focus. You'll also gain insight into the essence of Bombay Sapphire, followed by a cocktail at the Bombay Sapphire bar, of course (just don't ask to mix it with tonic!). Illegal in the US but not in the UK, Absinthe is great way to end the tour. A little bit of this green liquor, known as the "green fairy", is enough to make your mind swim even more. A tour so fun you must be hallucinating. Oh that's right, you are. **Crowd** All kinds of people are attracted to this museum. On a Friday afternoon, you will be among plenty of business types winding down after a hard week of work. **Prices** Three tour packages: Classic (£12.50) - 5 tastings and one Bombay Sapphire. Premium - same as Classic but add two premium wine tastings and a course on how to taste wine. Ultimate - 10 wine tastings, How to taste wine, 4 premium wine tastings, 2 shots of Absinthe, Bombay Sapphire cocktail, and 2 premium coffee tastings. **Web Site** www.vinopolis.co.uk **Dress** No dress code. **Hot Nights/When to Go** Go later to jumpstart the night. Last tour is 2 hours before closing. **Close By** *Little bar/cantina*: Right at the Vinopolis entrance, has a huge wine list and rustic Old French feel. *Wine Warf* : A more modern and upscale wine bar that you can go to halfway through the tour if you want. *Bourogh Street Market*: A large, open-air market that can be fun to walk around; lots of fresh fruits, vegetables, and even more wine. *The Majestic*: A wine shop attached to Vinopolis. Get wine here from all over world at all different prices. *Market Porter:* Sick of drinking wine? This old style pub with oak barrels for tables is on Stony St.

LONDONOTHER

Tip from Tuck: "If you really want to get drunk here, it may be best to spring for the ultimate package. You get the most and save £5 overall. The ultimate tour lasts for hours, and make sure you don't miss anything. After you go through the tour, make your way over to the Market Porter Pub to keep the party going!"

PARIS

The Party Climate:

Despite rumors of smug, arrogant Parisians, these locals are the heart and soul of a vibrant social scene. Though you may meet the occasional snob, Parisians, in general, are friendly, willing to help when you lose your way, and will not mind too much when you fumble with their language; they may even be interested in talking with you. Their party-haven promises fun for visitors of any age, disposition, or budget (almost), if only you know where to look. Because there is truly no experience quite as enchanting as Paris in early summer and fall, the City of Light attracts visitors (more than any other city in the world) like a beacon, reflecting all of the brilliance to be found within. Rich in culture, tradition, romance, and hedonism (all important elements of an intense social scene), Paris can and will live up to its grandiose reputation if you embrace its pace, its personality, and its joie de vivre.

By day, Paris offers some incredible sights that you simply cannot miss. You won't find it hard to fill your time with amazing shopping, great cafés, or simply strolling the Champs-Elysées. While away the daytime hours in a cozy Latin Quarter café or grab a picnic and a bottle of wine to enjoy beneath the Eiffel Tower before ascending to the top for some amazing views, but whatever you do, don't hurry. Take in the charm of Paris' parks and avenues by day, and you'll be ready for the nighttime frivolity.

The nightlife here is cosmopolitan, chic, and often very expensive. After a slow start on Monday and Tuesday nights, the festivity begins to build on Wednesday and grows to a feverish pitch on Friday and Saturday nights when the parties tend to last until sun up. You should plan your visit accordingly. Paris' more posh and exclusive clubs have a 20-euro cover charge on the weekends, which usually includes one drink. Guys must understand, however, that 20 euros doesn't guarantee entry into the hippest nightspots (especially if they can tell that you are American)…it is necessary to show up with girls, as many as possible. Posh clubs love to fill their dance floors with pretty girls who fit right in with their hip décor and refined atmosphere. If sipping expensive drinks at sophisticated clubs isn't your thing, there are plenty of more casual and economical choices among Parisian bars. Whether in one of the pulsating clubs or a more laid back American bar, Paris at night is diverse and captivating.

Our Overall Impressions:

Tucker - 2
"If only I had studied my French in school, I could actually communicate with some of these people, especially the French girls. Instead, I find myself gravitating towards those bars that are primarily English speaking. Luckily, the American bars and Irish pubs in France are a ton of fun. With completely laid back and casual atmospheres, they are usually filled with friendly people to whom I can relate. I think they are a much better diversion than the fancy clubs that sometimes seem to look down on me because I'm American and won't let me inside if I show up without a girl."

Adam - 3
"I love to listen to live music and chill out, which I am able to in some interesting areas of Paris, like Montmartre. And the days here are great; I can hang out at beautiful parks and enjoy some intense people watching. If you can catch Le Fete de la Musique, a free city-wide music festival that takes place every June 21, your trip to Paris will be even more worthwhile. You can hang out with some very cool Parisians who you would never find any other night of the year, and they are happy to share a piece of their culture and some refreshment with a new friend."

"Whatever you do, don't leave Paris without tasting at least one Banana Nutella Crepe (3.5 euros most places). Miss this and deprive yourself of the tastiest late night snack ever."

Brittney - 4
"Paris is everything I expected and so much more. I had heard good things about the shopping, but it is, in fact, amazing. I feel right at home in Paris' classy and sophisticated clubs, and I love prowling for famous people. The scene at night is so welcoming and vibrant. Of course, I am a girl, so all of the doors are open to me, even places on the Champs-Elysées. This city is so alive!"

Emma - 3
"With all of its attractions and intrigue, Paris is quite expensive. Nevertheless, even I can have a great time, take in some of the most incredible sights in the world, meet lots of people, and keep my spending under control. Some of the bars offer great Happy hour deals and cheap drinks throughout the night, and as a girl, I am often able to dodge the cover charge at fancy clubs. Mostly though, I enjoy the very good and very cheap wine. You can find me most nights at sunset with a bottle of wine and my friends in a park."

Our Perfect Days/Nights:

Brittney:
"In the world's most fashionable city, how else would I spend my day but shopping. Working my way down from rue St. Honore toward the Champs-Elysées, I would stop by the Buddha Bar for a little lunch and maybe a cocktail before hitting Hermes and the Arc de Triumph (which I find to be equally inspiring Parisian attractions). By night, I would hit the hottest spots in Paris. **Man Ray**, owned by Johnny Depp and Sean Penn, is pricey but worth every penny for the sophisticated scene. After dinner and drinks, I would continue the party at **Bar Fly** (if it's good enough for Usher, it's good enough for me) and with dancing until dawn at the **Latina Café**. There are plenty of posh clubs that strike my fancy along the Champs, so plans could change."

Tucker:
Day - sleep late, Champs-Elysées
Night - Dinner and wine beneath the Eiffel tower, Top of the Eiffel Tower, Le Violin
Dingue, Banana Nutella Crepe

Adam:
Day- Buttes-Chaumot, Art Gallery by Sacre Coure
Night - Le Bazar Egyptien, Top of Eiffel Tower, Le Violin
Dingue, Banana Nutella Crepe

Emma:
Day - Rue Mouffetard, Champs-Elysées
Night- Picnic with wine by the Eiffel Tower, Top of the Eiffel Tower, Favela Chic

Our Top 5 Spots:

Tucker
1. Le Violin Dingue
2. Nighttime Picnic before ascending the Eiffel Tower
3. Buddha Bar
4. Man Ray
5. Larry Flint Hustler Club

Adam
1. Fete de la Musique (June 21)
2. Le Bazar Egyptien
3. Le Violin Dingue
4. Nighttime Picnic before ascending the Eiffel Tower
5. Le Distillerie

Brittney
1. Man Ray
2. Buddha Bar
3. Le Violin Dingue
4. Barrio Latino
5. Rue St. Honore

Emma
1. Nighttime Picnic before ascending the Eiffel Tower
2. Rue Mouffetard
3. Favela Chic
4. Le Violin Dingue
5. Bus Palladium (Tuesday nights free for girls - drinks and all!)

Hotspots by Night of the Week:

	Mon	Tu	Wed	Th	F	Sa	Su
	Latina Café	Frog and Princess	Sanz Sans	Le Violin Dingue	Man Ray	Buddha Bar	Larry Flint Hustler Club
	Le Who's Bar	Le Bazar Egyptien	Eiffel Tower	Le Distillerie	China Club	Le Violin Dingue	River Bar
	Café Mabillon	Bus Palladium	Le Violin Dingue	Buddha Bar	Barrio Latino	Man Ray	Bar Fly
	Eiffel Tower night	Bus Palladium	Le 10 Bar	Le Violin Dingue	Latina Café	Favela Chic	Bob Cool

Neighborhoods -
The Social Landscape:

Bastille/Oberkampf (11eme): Because of its diversity and energy, the 11eme may be the most fun and social area in which to hang out in Paris. Bars are prevalent in the Bastille area, and they exude cultural influence. There is, therefore, something for everyone here. Along rue du Faubourg St. Antoine, you'll find upscale yet inviting dance clubs and lounges attracting a sophisticated crowd. The narrow, cobblestone, parallel street, du Lappe, is lined with bars, many of which offer live music to complement their cultural vibe. Whether you are smoking from a hookah at **Le Bazar Egyptian** or having your Taro cards read at **Le Bar Sans Nom**, you'll be struck by the international flair here and will enjoy the variety it affords you.

If you are looking for a genuinely French experience in the 11eme, head to Oberkampf. Although you won't find many English speakers here, you can catch a glimpse of the underground scene that offers some insight into the local social life and an escape from the tourists. You'll be a minority here for sure, but the locals seem happy to converse with the occasional American. With plenty of entertainment from bars, to concerts, to clubs, this area is worthy of a visit if you have the time.

Champs- Elysées (8eme): Although this is the most expensive area in all of Paris, you can enjoy the Champs-Elysées by day without sabotaging your budget. Replete with upscale stores, charming cafes, and interesting people, the Champs Elysées invites you to linger over a coffee and survey the parade of locals and tourists ambling by.

After sunset, however, is another story entirely. The bars and clubs lining this famous avenue, while doing their part to keep the party going until the sun comes up, charge a pricey fee to do so. The clubs are classy, chic, and considered by locals to be among the city's best. So, if you have the money to spend and are here after dark, dance the night away at a swanky club. If you are more interested in meeting people and hanging out in an "American-style" bar atmosphere, hit a nearby watering hole (like **House of Live** or **Bar Fly**) for a spirited atmosphere and friendly crowds.

The Latin Quarter (5eme/6eme): By day and night, the lively Latin Quarter has a pulse all its own, one that seems to emerge from its young, somewhat artsy student population. It is young and less posh, exclusive, and expensive than much of Paris. With irreverence to the pricey club scene, it bustles with tiny cafes, bookstores, and bars, representing the eclectic tastes of the neighborhood and the international flavor of the city. Although its exact boundaries are debatable, its appeal to young American travelers is not. Whether you are up for relaxing cocktails by the river at **Polly Magoo's**, funky live music at **La Who's Bar**, or a taste of home (not to be missed) at **Le Violin Dingue**, the Latin Quarter is definitely worth checking out.

Marais (3eme/4eme): This neighborhood offers a vivid taste of Paris' nightlife with a number of cool, low-key bars. Though the Marais gives off a hint of a hippie, alternative vibe, the bars here tend to be International and play all kinds of music. By day, you'll find plenty of quaint yet hip cafes and bistros, as well as a multitude of unique shopping opportunities. The vintage stores here are spectacular. Rue Vieille-du-Temple, especially, represents the center of gay Paris and is a great area to soak in a true Euro vibe.

Montmartre (18eme): Adjacent to Pigalle, Montmartre is an intriguing mix of the tasteful/chic and the seedy. Charming and with a bohemian feel to it, this neighborhood is home to many of the city's infamous cabarets and nightclubs, as well as some diverse shopping. The party atmosphere is festive and inviting, if only to experience its dichotomy.

Pigalle (9eme): Pigalle, the city's most mischievous neighborhood, is essentially the red light district of Paris. Walking along strip club and sex shop lined streets, you will continually be propositioned to enter these shady establishments. Don't. No matter what the time or your state of mind, you will basically be robbed. Despite this less than glamorous situation, this neighborhood does have its share of fun bars and clubs/cabarets that party all night long on the weekends. Although the haunts of Pigalle are certainly not among the most sophisticated in Paris, they do offer funky and energetic scenes and an eclectic crowd. Some, like **O'Sullivans**, are more English speaking, less techno-focused, and are even great places to meet people.

BASTILLE/OBERKAMPF

Bar de Familles

Bar	19 R. de Lappe	**Night**
Daily from 6pm-2am		

😊 4 😊 3 😊 1 😊 3

The Scene This small, unassuming neighborhood bar may not look like much, but it could be the best spot to catch any major sporting event. The giant projection screen (perhaps Paris' largest) surrounded by a semi-circle of seats enables you and your friends to catch all the action. If France happens to be playing soccer at the time, this venue will be packed with screaming fans. The atmosphere is lively with the spirit of competition. Come here for the cheap beers and sports on TV. **Crowd** The sports-watching crowd tends to be primarily guys, and no one here is afraid to get rowdy. Folks are friendly as long as the home team is winning. **Food/Misc** They advertise Sunday night NFL football. **Prices** Pints of beer start at €4, Guinness only €6, mixed drinks €5, shots €3. **Dress** Casual. **Hot Nights/When to Go** Anytime there is a game on TV that you just can't miss.

Tip from Tuck: "If there is a game you want to watch, come here early to get a place in front of the big screen. Otherwise, you will have to be cramped while watching the game on a small screen over the bar. The beer is cheap, so don't worry if you have to stay a while."

Barrio Latino

Bar/restaurant	46-48 R. du Faubourg Saint Antoine	**Night**
Su-Th 11:30pm-2am, F-Sa open until 3am		Day

😊 3 😊 2 😊 4 😊 2

The Scene Like an old Spanish or Cuban Mansion, Barrio Latino provides four floors of luxury. The feel is open, grand, and lavish, as the three upper floors are comprised simply of balconies. So, standing on the first floor, let your eyes wander to the top and take in this unique space. Although this is a perfect place to lounge during the day, the weekends are lively and full of energy with a huge crowd dancing to house and Latin music. They have spared no expense giving patrons the feel and style of old-time elegance with antique looking furniture and spectacular attention to detail, while reminiscent of everyone's favorite gangster, Tony Montana. **Crowd** The crowd here is a mix…from young people looking to let loose to older men with lots of money, fancy things and beautiful ladies surrounding them. Whatever the case, you must look good and bring some sophistication to the scene. **Entertainment/Music** They offer salsa-dancing classes during the week. **Food/Misc** Nuevo Latino cuisine, which means they serve tapas. **Prices** Mixed drinks are €9.50, cocktails start at €10, and €61 for a liter jug, beers are €8 for a pint, €5.50 for bottles, wine starts at €4 a glass, €16.50 for a bottle. Cover is €8 Thursdays-Saturday. **Dress** Dressy. **Hot Nights/When to Go** Arrive around 10:30pm to avoid having to wait in line all night.

Tip from Brittney: "Barrio Latino has tons of class and refined guests…a great place to see and be seen. On the weekends, the line can be hundreds of people long, so get here early and look beautiful."

Café Charbon

Bar	109 R. d'Oberkampf	Night
Daily 9am-2am		

 2   3   1   3

The Scene A melding of old and new occurs in this intriguing French café. The structure and detailed wood paneling seem original, but Charbon's interior has a modern feel. Paintings near the ceiling are a clever reminder of how Parisians at the turn of the 19th century liked to party and enjoy life. Patrons also are a mixture of young and old and they maintain a lively atmosphere with local flavor…the most energy of any place on the street. **Crowd** Patrons who hang out here are French primarily. Some of them have a little bit of an alternative edge, while others look like they just got out of work. Expect to find a mix of local personalities and friendly folk. **Entertainment/Music** American Rock music playing in the background is not the focus here. **Food/Misc** Offers a full menu with all sorts of food from beef to chicken and lots of desserts. **Prices** Small glass of wine for €2.80, cocktail of the day €5.50, beers €4.70. Happy hour from 5-7pm with beers for €3.50. 140cl beer (almost 3 pints) for €11. Meals start at €11 up to €34. After 9:30pm, all drink prices increase by €0.50. **Dress** Casual.
Hot Nights/When to Go Come here for dinner and a few drinks before heading next door to Nuevo Casino.

Tip from Adam: "I am a little confused here. Do they want to create an old, authentic Parisian bar feel or a modern trendy hangout? Either way, good food and a mix of people lead to a good time here."

Favela Chic

Club	16 R. du Faubourg-du-Temple	Night
Tu-Sa 8pm-2am		

2   2   3   4

The Scene A Brazilian style dance club that is just as hot and sweaty as you would expect. The mood here is feverish, as young people find anywhere and way they can to let loose in this packed club. Girls here show off seductive dance moves to Latin and Brazilian beats as guys stare in awe, angling to get closer to the action. You won't find a club more dynamic and energetic than this, so if you are not prepared for a night on the dance floor, this is not the place for you. A tiny slice of the hot Brazilian style of partying. **Crowd** Lots of girls (all young…30 and under) come here because they love the music, and they love to dance with each other. The music seems to overtake the crowd as they dance the night away. **Entertainment/Music** Latin and Brazilian music. The DJ also likes to play hip-hop with added Brazilian beats. **Food/Misc** Live Brazilian music on Tuesday and Wednesday nights. **Prices** €10 cover charge on the weekends includes one drink, cocktails €9, beers start at €5. **Dress** Casual. **Hot Nights/When to Go** Busiest on the weekends. The line starts forming around 11pm, so arrive earlier to avoid the wait.

Tip from Emma: "Be prepared to work up a sweat here. If you want to cool off, the best place is at the bar where the fans hit your face. Come here with your girlfriends for a night of crazy fun and dancing."

Kitty's Irish Pub	Pub/Café	4 R. de la Roquette	**Night**
	Daily 4pm - 2am		

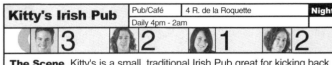

3 2 1 2

The Scene Kitty's is a small, traditional Irish Pub great for kicking back with a pint. Many locals relax here, and it's a great spot to find some friendly English-speaking folks. With an atmosphere that is simple and cozy, without any flashy, commercial feel whatsoever, conversation flows easily, so don't be shy. They serve authentic Irish food too, so check this place out around happy hour. **Crowd** All ages mix here…relaxed, inviting, and friendly people…very conversational.
Entertainment/Music Classic rock, Irish music, etc. **Food/Misc** Happy hour 6-9pm daily (reduced prices), grilled meats, Irish breakfast, etc. 8-10 €s. **Prices** Beers €4-6, spirits €4-5, cocktails €6-7.50. **Dress** Completely casual. **Hot Nights/When to Go** Thursday through Sunday for happy hour or around 11pm.

Tip from Tuck: "It's nice to find a small, simple pub once in awhile to have a pint with friends. Come here for a reasonable dinner and start the night off with good conversation and cheap beers."

PARIS BASTILLE/OBERKAMPF

La Fabrique	Club	53 R. du Faubourg St Antoine	**Night**
	Daily 10am-5am		Day

3 2 3 2

The Scene This unique restaurant/club combo serves great food all day long and then dishes out premium cocktails into the twilight hours. La Fabrique is appealing in that it isn't an overwhelming, massive club, but rather a quaint, intimate establishment with a style of its own. The dance floor is in the back with a number of private booths/tables next to it, in case you just want to chill out and watch the dance action. One long bar in the front of the club serves all, but it can get crowded around 12:30am as patrons gain momentum. Soft blue lights illuminate the scene as a friendly crowd drinks, dances, and forgets their worries.
Crowd A mid-20s to late 30s stylish and well-dressed crowd seems to be excited and happy to be here. **Entertainment/Music** Great DJs turning tables…house techno, dance, and hip-hop beats. **Food/Misc** Appetizers €6-11, entrees €12-15 (meats, pastas, variety of French foods). **Prices** Beer €8, cocktails €9-11, shooters €5. No cover before 11pm and €8 (which includes a drink) afterwards. **Web Site** www.subvitamine.com **Dress** Club attire. **Hot Nights/When to Go** Gets going around 12:30/1am on the weekends.

Tip from Brittney: "Come here before 11pm, and you won't even have to pay to get in. You'll like the friendly young people you meet here, and if you're just looking to drink and dance with some friends, then this place is perfect for that too."

Le Bar Sans Nom

Bar	49 R. de Lappe	**Night**
M-Th 7pm-2am, F-Sa until 4am		Day

👤 2   👤 2   👤 3   👤 3

PARIS BASTILLE/OBERKAMPF

The Scene Le Bar Sans Nom envelops you with a certain mysticism as you enter through an exotic red veil. With an eclectic mix of old, unique, and mix-matched furniture and walls donning large tapestries, the atmosphere here is intriguing. Couches with fluffy pillows allow you to sink right in and accept the calm spirit surrounding you here. Come on Tuesday nights for free Taro card readings, a glimpse into your past and that of your ancestors. A welcoming and mystical atmosphere makes it a neat spot to hang out and make some new friends.
Crowd The patrons here hail from all over the world and range in age from 18-80 years, so you can meet any kind of person. Patrons tend to be very spiritual, mystical, and interested in who you are. They create a relaxed atmosphere where you never feel out of place.
Entertainment/Music Music of all kinds here, but it plays primarily in the background, as this is a bar for meeting and talking with others.
Food/Misc Free Taro card readings on Tuesday nights. **Prices** Beer starts at €5, mixed drinks start at €6.20, long drinks €8.50, shots start at €6.20. **Dress** Casual. **Hot Nights/When to Go** Tuesday night for the Taro card reading and weekends are the busiest.

Tip from Emma: "On Tuesday nights, come here for the free Taro card readings and learn all about your past. They don't tell you your future though, because that is for you to decide."

Le Bataclan

Pub/Café	50 Blvd. Voltaire	**Night**
Depends on who is playing		

👤 4   👤 4   👤 2   👤 3

The Scene La Bataclan has much potential as a great place to catch a show, depending on who the act is. Although it is a small concert venue, they have hosted the likes of Prince and many other renowned performers and provide an intimate arena. The open general admission area allows the crowd to be up close and personal with the performers, while a balcony with seating all the way around provides another perspective. The bar in the back offers somewhat of a respite from the craziness near the stage. **Crowd** The crowd is determined entirely by who the performer is. **Entertainment/Music** Depends on the night, but catch a good band, and this could be a lot of fun. **Prices** Ticket prices depend on who is playing. Mixed drinks start at €7, beers for €4, but they only serve half-pints. **Dress** Casual.
Hot Nights/When to Go Hit is when there is a band you want to see. Call 0143143535 to see who is playing.

Tip from Adam: "I love live music, and this venue is small and gets some sweet acts. If you are in Paris for a while, make sure to check out who is coming. After the show, head to the café next door to enjoy a few drinks"

Le Bazar Egyptian

Restaurant	29/31 R. de Lappe	**Night**
Tu-Su 4pm-2am		Day

👤 3   👤 4   👤 3   👤 3

The Scene A fun and captivating spot to escape the typical Parisian bar or restaurant scene, unlike any other in Paris. This Egyptian restaurant maintains a completely authentic feel from the food right down to the costumes of the waiters and waitresses. The walls display an incredible array of colorful detailed patterns to enhance the atmosphere, along with the distinct brown stone wall with tiny cascading waterfalls. The best area in which to hang out is definitely the shisha (hookah) bar - a separate room with a luxurious fluffy couch wrapping its perimeter and golden engraved tabletops, as well as more beautiful and complex patterns and paintings of modern Egyptian themes. Patrons enjoy smoking and sipping tea in this comfortable haven to relax after dinner. **Crowd** The shisha bar gets crowded with young people looking to chill after a nice meal. Although this spot is upscale, anybody is welcome. **Entertainment/Music** On Tuesday and Wednesday nights, there is Egyptian belly dancing. **Food/Misc** The food here is all authentic Egyptian. **Prices** €12 for shisha lasts for 1 hour, beers €3.50-5, mixed drinks €7, bottles of wine start €19. Happy Hour from 4-8pm: drinks start at €3.50. Appetizers start at €8, entrées at €18, Tajines for €16. **Dress** Casual. **Hot Nights/When to Go** Come here for dinner or even just to smoke from the shisha. Anytime can be fun, as long you come with a group.

Tip from Adam: "Best idea is to come with a group of friends and hang out in the shisha room. After eating, this is an amazing place to chill out and take in a different scene. Drink some tea and smoke some flavored tobacco."

Le Blue Billiard

Other	111 R. Saint-Maur	**Night**
Daily 12pm-2am		

👤 3   👤 3   👤 0   👤 1

The Scene If you are struck by the urge to hang out and play pool, this is the place for you. Le Blue Billiard offers nine regular sized American-style pool tables, which are hard to find in Paris. Although the scene is not very lively, it's not a bad place to grab a few pints and shoot some pool with the locals. The atmosphere, not surprisingly, is that of a dark pool hall frequented by hustlers trying to win some cash. You can avoid playing them. A bar at the front of the pool hall pays tribute to Blues greats such as BB King, Robert Johnson, and the Blues Brothers. **Crowd** The crowd that comes here is primarily interested in playing pool and hanging out. They are very casual and mostly local. **Entertainment/Music** Even though they commemorate jazz greats, they like to play famous music from the 1970s and early 80s. **Food/Misc** 19 Pool Tables, 9 of which are American-style. **Prices** Bottled beers start at €4.50, cocktails start at €7.50, mixed drinks start at €7. €12 charge for one hour of pool. **Dress** Completely casual. **Hot Nights/When to Go** Whenever you feel like playing pool.

Tip from Tuck: "Don't expect to find a ton of people here to meet, but if you want to play a few games of pool and take it easy one night, this is the place to do just that."

Le Distillerie	Theme bar	50 R. du Faubourg St-Antoine	Night
	M-Th 7pm-4am, F-Sa 7pm-5am		

The Scene This little bar/club/restaurant will transport you to the Caribbean. Complete with topical décor, including plants and a tiki bar, groovy African/Caribbean tunes, and rustic wicker furniture, the feel here is completely authentic. You might even find yourself looking around for the turquoise waters of the sea. A back room offers additional seating and a cozy setting, especially on the weekend when La Distillerie gets really packed. During the week, this is a fun spot to enjoy fruity drinks, happy music, and a lively atmosphere. **Crowd** A young, eclectic crowd in their 20s and 30s enjoys the music and the laid-back, Caribbean style here. **Entertainment/Music** African/Caribbean tunes…DJs Thursday-Saturday. **Food/Misc** Starters (fish, salads, etc.) for €6, main dishes €9-14 (chicken curry, beef in peanut sauce, seafood, etc.). **Prices** Coffee €2-3, wine €5, cocktails €8, punch €6, mixed drinks €8, shots €7, small beers €4.5, tropical juice €4. **Web Site** www.ladistillerie-bar.com **Dress** Smart Casual. **Hot Nights/When to Go** Thursday-Saturday for the DJ.

Tip from Adam: "Great music, real chill, cool staff, definitely worth coming by for a night. Enjoy the tropical drinks and the groovy ambiance here."

Nouveau Casino	Bar/club	109 R. Oberkampf	**Night**
	Depends on the event		

👨 3   👩 4   👩 3   👩 3

The Scene Nouveau Casino is located in an area in which many locals who are part of the "underground" scene like to hang out. There is different kind of entertainment here almost every night, but most of the time, the place is dedicated to either being a club or a concert venue. Therefore, the scene changes frequently; however, they do get some of the best acts from town and all over Europe. If you want to party in a different area of town, check out the website to see if anything here is for you. **Crowd** The crowd changes nightly along with the acts. For the most part, the patrons here are going to be locals and like to stay away from the big and trendy clubs. **Entertainment/Music** Varies by night. **Web Site** www.nouveaucasino.net **Dress** Smart-casual. **Hot Nights/When to Go** Can be good any night; it just depends on what is going on.

Tip from Adam: "With all sorts of different live music, Nouveau Casino is definitely worth checking out to see if there is something here that interests you."

PARIS BASTILLE/OBERKAMPF

Nun's Café	Bar	112 R. Saint Maur	**Night**
	Daily 5pm -2am		Day

👨 2   👩 3   👩 0   👩 3

The Scene Sometimes a bar relies on its vibe and unique atmosphere to attract patrons, and other times, it's the people who make the bar. Nun's Café is one of these places...a spot to escape the scene and get to know some real Parisians. This place is a little gem of a watering hole where people in the underground scene hang out. The friendly atmosphere stems from the feeling that everyone at the bar has been coming here for years and has grown up together. But, they will welcome you in a second. Don't worry about what it looks like; just come to meet some friendly folk and to enjoy the best Mojito you'll ever have. **Crowd** A real local crowd hangs out here on the weekends and, especially, during happy hour. They appear to be writers or artistic types who are super-friendly and happy that you have come to their little hang out. **Entertainment/Music** The bartender plays the music, which seems to be her own CD collection from home. Led Zeppelin may be her favorite, but the real entertainment is the bar's patrons.
Food/Misc They don't serve food, but run next door to the Indian restaurant, and he will gladly bring over some dinner for you.
Prices Happy Hour everyday from 5-9:30pm, Pint of Amstel €3, half pint €1.50, cocktails €6.50. **Dress** Completely casual.
Hot Nights/When to Go During Happy Hour, the bar gets a good crowd, and they have cheap beer. People will congregate here pretty much anytime of the night.

Tip from Adam: "When you are sick of your friends or perhaps are studying abroad in Paris, this bar can be fun even if you come alone. If you speak French, it's even better."

Sanz Sans

Bar/Club	49 R. du Faubourg St. Antoine	**Night**
Su-M 9am-1am, Tu-Sa 9am-5am		Day

4 | 3 | 3 | 3

PARIS BASTILLE/OBERKAMPF

The Scene This place definitely has a feel and style of its own. A large square bar greets you at the entrance with bustling dance floors to either side. Around back, you'll find the restaurant section of this club with tons of tables and even an upstairs balcony seating area. You can't miss the huge black & white movie screen on the back wall revealing the dance floor's secrets. Loud, groovy music gets you moving, whether on the floor or just in your chair. Dim red lights illuminate the bar, and hanging cymbals encourage the bartenders to break out some drumsticks and add to this club's already great tunes. **Crowd** A young and hip crowd in their early 20s to late 30s frequents this spot. Folks are friendly with a lot of energy. **Entertainment/Music** DJs spinning hip-hop, techno, and funky dance beats. **Prices** No cover charge, beer €4-4.50, cocktails €9. **Web Site** www.sanzsans.com **Dress** Smart Casual…stylish. **Hot Nights/When to Go** F/Sa.

Tip from Tuck: "This place is great because there is no hassle at the door, the ladies are cute, and the patrons are fairly normal. It's a great club for those who are looking to just party, meet people, and not get bumped around by crazy ravers."

Wax

Bar/club	15 R. Daval	**Night**
Tu-Th 6pm-2am, F and Sa 6pm-6am, closed Su		

3 | 3 | 4 | 4

The Scene The fun retro feel at Wax makes it a great spot to dance the night away with friends old and new. The pinkish glow enveloping the bar, along with the brightly painted swirls on the columns and red disco balls, take patrons back to the 1970s. We love to lounge here early in the night in the ultra-chic chairs you can actually climb inside of. On the weekends, enjoy the DJ spinning for the lively dance floor throughout the night until 6am. The authentic retro atmosphere will make you feel like you should be wearing bell-bottom pants and a button down with a huge collar. **Crowd** The crowd here is very casual and wants to be at a lounge to relax and escape the swanky Parisian clubs. Patrons don't take themselves too seriously, so meeting people should not be a problem. **Entertainment/Music** DJ battles on some nights. They play house techno most the time, but any kind of dance music goes here. **Prices** No cover charge. Beer starts at €4.50, mixed drinks €7.50, and cocktails €9. **Web Site** www.wax.fr **Dress** Casual.
Hot Nights/When to Go On the weekends, this place is not going to get crowded until 12am, but it goes on all night.

Tip from Brittney: "The fabulous 1970 décor makes this place well worth the visit. The retro-style chairs they have are unreal."

CHAMPS-ELYSÉES

Barfly

Bar	49/51 Av. George V	**Night**
Daily 12pm-2:30am		

👨 4 👩 2 👩 4 👩 2

The Scene Right off the Champs, Barfly lives up to the fine reputation of its surroundings. Upon entering, you'll find one extremely long bar running almost the entire length of the wall. Antonio Gaudi style mosaic tiles cover the bar, and red velvet bar stools and booths are scattered about the beautiful hardwood floor. Glowing red modern art adorns one wall, while a gigantic stone statue rests by some of the tables. Out front is a quaint patio enclosed with greenery, and in the back, you'll find a sushi bar and more tables, as well as a mini DJ booth set upon a small balcony. The candles on each table, the chandeliers, and the sophisticated decor make this an uppity, posh bar - even for Paris. Very swanky and elite, yet a fun and exciting spot to grab some drinks.
Crowd The somewhat arrogant, well-dressed, and stylish crowd is mid-20s and up. **Entertainment/Music** It varies, but classy house/techno music generally keeps the mood here elevated.
Food/Misc Fixed dinner menu for €24, brunch on Sunday €34, starters €14-15, entrees €17-22, sushi/sashimi €6-15. **Prices** Beers €7-8, cocktails €10-12, smoothies €10. **Dress** Smart Casual to dressy.
Hot Nights/When to Go Gets really packed Saturday at 12:30am.

Tip from Tuck: "This place is high-class and fun. It's great though, because they don't charge a cover. So, come here as a transition from a typical bar to a nightclub. Be sure to look good though."

Buddha Bar

Bar	8/12 R. Boissy d'Anglais	**Night**
Su-Th 6pm-2am, F-Sa 6pm-3am		

👨 4 👩 3 👩 4 👩 2

The Scene You'll notice the Buddhist focus of this place immediately, as colorful flowers and miniature statues of tigers and Buddhas adorn the entrance. As you walk down the stairs, however, the real experience of the Buddha bar begins. A balcony bar overlooking the dining room is virtually pitch black, except for the dim white glow of candles scattered about. Although the place comes alive on the weekends as a diverse crowd dances around the bar to Arabian techno, the tranquility never diminishes. A mood so peaceful that you can't help but be relaxed here. **Crowd** The crowd is sophisticated, chic, and has plenty of money to spend. The age range is from around 25-50 years, and to fit in, you need to be well dressed, sophisticated, and, of course, properly bathed. **Entertainment/Music** During the evening, they play soothing lounge music. On the weekends at midnight, the DJ starts to play some house music described as Arabian techno. **Food/Misc** A 40-foot statue of the Buddha in meditation dominates the restaurant, and a 100-foot bar has a huge dragon's head at one end and a tail at the other. The restaurant downstairs is very expensive, so you may want to stick to the bar where they serve all kinds of sushi. **Prices** Cocktails start at €8, shots are €8, glasses of wine starts at €9. Sushi prices: 1 piece for €3.50, 3 pieces for €5, 5 pieces for €9. **Web Site** buddha.bar@buddha-bar.fr **Dress** Dressy. **Hot Nights/When to Go** The weekends are the most crowded. Come here around 10:30pm to get a table.

Tip from Tuck: "This place is so soothing, like a massage without the happy ending."

Champs Elysées	Outdoor activity		**Night**
	All day and night		Day

3 3 4 3

The Scene A visitor to Paris has to check out the Champs-Elysees. Although an expensive area in which to eat and drink, it offers an amazing environment in which to hang out, do some people-watching, and window shop. Thousands of people, mostly tourists, wander the street appreciating the French flair so abundant here or, perhaps, making their way to the Arc du Triumph. Many familiar retail stores line the Champs selling anything from clothing to music. Peugeot and Mercedes showrooms offer entertainment for auto enthusiasts, as they showcase cars of the present and future. The sidewalk here is exceptionally wide and bustling with a variety of outdoor cafes. A walk on the Champs-Elysées seems to bring history to life, while offering a unique glimpse into current fashion trends. Simply put, you will feel like you are somewhere significant, and you are. **Crowd** Tourists of all ages and from every country visit here. It seems possible to hear almost any language imaginable. Depending on their destination, visitors here may be dressed to the 9s or simply in shorts and a t-shirt. **Food/Misc** There are a great variety of food options along the Champs-Elysées. Although some spots tend to be a bit less expensive than their upscale neighbors, most here will cost a pretty penny. **Dress** Anything you want. **Hot Nights/When to Go** During the day and even in the evening, there will always be people to see and meet. **Close By** There are places to eat and drink all along the Champs. *Deli's Café* has sandwiches starting at €4 for take away. The *Cottage Elysees* is just off the main road and has an Irish pub feel mixed with some French flavor. *House of Live* is close by with live rock music at night. Across from House of Live is a bar that is open 24 hours a day. Finally, *Café Montecristo* offers Happy hour specials from 3-8pm and some cigars to go along with it.

Tip from Tuck: "Although almost every girl is going to come here for the shopping, try to avoid it unless Brittney is dragging you along. The best pastime for guys is to check out the two car showrooms for a little while. Beyond that, *Virgin Records* is always worth killing some time in. The Deli's Cafe is one of the cheaper places to get some food to take with you, and House of Live is great spot to grab a beer and get off the Champs."

House of Live	Bar	124 R. La Boetie	**Night**
	Daily 9am-5am		

4　3　3　3

The Scene The atmosphere here is that of an American bar, not a brasserie. With no seating on the street, the main attraction of House of Live is…the live music. Bands are primarily French, but they play American style rock and even sing in English most of the time. When a large crowd gathers, they open up the downstairs area, which resembles a tiny pool hall. The atmosphere here is friendly and welcoming to Americans. Many here speak English, which makes it easier to carry on a conversation with a local or meet some new friends.
Crowd The age range is 21-35. Tourists and locals mix with great regularity here due to the location. A very casual crowd, the kind you might expect at a bar with rock music. **Entertainment/Music** Live rock music here daily starting from 11-11:30pm and going until after midnight. W-Sa, they have a DJ until closing. Su, they offer brunch and what is called New Soul music, which is kind of like gospel.
Food/Misc Known for its fajitas, primarily a Tex-Mex menu with a mix of traditional French food. **Prices** No cover, so the music is always free. Beers start at €3.90, cocktails €8.40. **Web Site** www.houseoflive.com
Dress Casual. **Hot Nights/When to Go** F/Sa are by far the best times, and it sometimes gets good on Thursdays as well. Come at 11pm for the live music.

Tip from Tuck: "I feel at home here. The live music is great; the people are fun, and you can stay all night. The best way to start a conversation is to ask where someone is from, followed by the "do you know so-and-so" game, followed by lying if you don't actually know anyone from her area. Seriously though, if you have no game, get a pint and play some pool."

Larry Flint's Hustler Club

	Other	13/15 R. de Berri	**Night**
	Daily 10pm -5am		

4　3　1　0

The Scene The Hustler brand has made its way to Paris, and tourists seem to be taking full advantage of it. This attraction is nothing less than a strip club with beautiful women on stage. Private shows are available as well. Although this is an expensive venture, it can be worth it, if you are into this sort of thing. Not a great place to meet people, but a different way to spend some time in the city. **Crowd** Lots of tourists come here, because they recognize the name and it seems appealing to them. You'll find guys of all ages; naturally, most are middle-aged. **Entertainment/Music** Topless strippers dancing on poles, and you will probably hear Van Halen's "I'm Hot for Teacher". **Prices** Cover charge of €25 includes one drink. Drinks are expensive after that. Private dance can be €100. **Web Site** www.hustlerclubparis.com **Dress** Wear something nice so you will be treated well.
Hot Nights/When to Go A night when nothing else is going on can be made lots of fun with a visit to the Hustler Club.

Tip from Tuck: "The Hustler Club is really expensive for a strip club, but it can be worth it for a fun time when nothing else is working out for you. Get at seat at the stage and smoke Marlboro Lights."

Latina Café

	Dance club	114 Av. des Champs-Elysées	**Night**
	Daily 11:30pm-6:30am		

4　3　4　3

The Scene You enter Latina Café from the Champs on a red carpet, and rightly so - you are entering quite a scene. The mood here is lively and fun almost any night of the week, but of course, it gets craziest on the weekends. Downstairs, a huge, bumping dance floor, surrounded by 2 bars and a balcony is the center of the action. Dim red lights illuminate the Latin-inspired décor of this club as loud, hip music gets everybody moving. With great cocktails, the bar gets crowded early. While you bust a move, be sure to check out the starry sky-view through the red-tinted skylight. **Crowd** A stylish and ethnic crowd in their early 20s to 30s loves to dance and mingle here. **Entertainment/Music** Loud, modern, hip dance music. **Food/Misc** Features a cool skylight you can look up through from the dance floor. **Prices** Cover charge on the weekends is €16, includes 2 drinks. During the week, guys pay €8, which includes 1 drink. Mojitos & cocktails for €10, glasses of wine for €4.5, beers for €5-6, shots for €7. **Dress** Smart-Casual to dressier. **Hot Nights/When to Go** Thursday through Saturday around 1am.

Tip from Emma: "This is a great place to go if you're looking to club during the week. Girls don't always have to pay a cover charge during the week, and I highly recommend the Mojitos!"

Le Queen

Club	102 Av. des Champs Elysées	**Night**
Daily 12am-late		

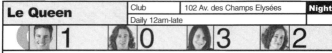

1 0 3 2

The Scene The entrance onto a balcony overlooking the dance floor at this vibrant club offers a great perspective on the action below. A large disco ball hangs above the floor providing mood lighting for the crowded space, and mirrors all around amplify the rowdiness surrounding you. The music and movement don't slow down here all night long, as the DJ pumps up an already enthusiastic crowd with techno and hip-hop. **Crowd** Gay men frequent this club, as well as girls. Even on nights when the crowd is supposed to be mixed, it is still a primarily gay crowd that likes to have fun, stay out late, and dance. **Entertainment/Music** Techno/hip-hop. **Food/Misc** Drinks are served with a lid and straw. **Prices** Cover charge of €10 includes one drink. Drinks are €9. **Dress** Casual club wear.
Hot Nights/When to Go Monday is straight night and Wednesday is mixed, but still mostly a gay club. If you want to stay out late in the middle of the week, you can do that here.

Tip from Brittney: "This club is fun but a little sketchy. May be hard to convince your group of friends to go here, but it promises to be a crazy time. I guess they put lids on the drinks to prevent girls from getting drugged."

Man Ray

Bar	34 R. Marbeuf	**Night**
M-Th 12pm-2am, F 12pm-5am, Sa-Su 6pm-5am		

4 4 4 3

The Scene Man Ray truly has no equal, and you can't miss the intriguing décor and ambiance here. This restaurant/bar/lounge resembles a massive Buddhist temple with serious Asian influence. The attention to detail is astonishing, as you'll find stained glass on the ceiling and the bar with light shining through. Huge wooden chandeliers hang from the high ceiling over the main floor, and a balcony encircles the entire place. Bars are upstairs and downstairs with modern art adorning the walls. Trendy island-style booths and a main stage with colorful flags hanging above it all contribute to the scene. The menu is exquisite, and this place screams extravagance. **Crowd** A bit of an older crowd in their mid-20s and up…a well-dressed and sophisticated mix of Parisians and visitors. **Entertainment/Music** DJ upstairs turns tables…all sorts of modern, hip, awesome music, depending on the theme of the night. **Food/Misc** Extensive, unique, trendy menu… lobster, caviar, Japanese, trendy seafood dishes. Starters for €15-20, main dishes €20 and up. **Prices** Cover charge of €20 on Friday and Saturday only. Beers €7, cocktails €11, mixed drinks €10.
Web Site www.manray.fr **Dress** Stylish club attire, chic.
Hot Nights/When to Go F/Sa night around midnight.

Tip from Brittney: "Just go check this place out on Friday or Saturday when it is open until 5am…you won't be disappointed. I've never seen a more lavish club than this, and it fills up with Paris' finest."

Pub Elysées Berry

Pub/Café	Entrance is at 2 R. de Berri	**Night**
Daily 8am- 5am		Day

👨 2   👩 3   👩 2   👩 3

The Scene This is a great bar for late night, especially during the week when a lot of places close down early. You can have a nightcap here in one of the booths or relax on the black sofas. A couple of TVs and lots of candlelight create an enjoyable atmosphere. You're also likely to find some tourists here. This intimate bar is great for meeting people after most others have gone to bed. Note that they do not serve food. **Crowd** A younger crowd in their 20s and 30s hits this spot…a mixture of locals and tourists. **Entertainment/Music** TVs… a pretty simple place. **Food/Misc** No food, beers from around the world, €1 supplement on all drink prices after 10pm. **Prices** Cocktails €7-9, €3-6 for glasses of wine. **Dress** Casual, though most here are dressed well. **Hot Nights/When to Go** F/Sa late (2 or 3am).

Tip from Emma: "When you're just not ready to call it quits on a night but almost every place has closed, you should come by Pub Elysées Berry. Great place to meet people, have a nightcap, and hang out late night without having to pay a cover at an expensive club."

Toi Bar & Restaurant

Restaurant	27 R. du Colisee	**Night**
Daily 12pm to 2am		Day

👨 2   👩 3   👩 3   👩 3

The Scene Toi is a very lush and trendy restaurant/bar with great atmosphere and a friendly feel. The downstairs is loaded with tables and loud, colorful decor. Upstairs, you'll find trendy seats/couches with pillows and additional tables. This venue looks and feels like something out of Soho, NY with its elaborate styling and trendy food/drink menu. Even the bathroom is beautifully colored, and sounds from the rainforest create a peaceful ambiance. **Crowd** A trendy, upscale, and chic crowd in their late 20s and up fills this spot. **Entertainment/Music** Trendy, soothing, melodic music. **Food/Misc** Main dishes (grilled beef, duck, tuna) €13-30, appetizers €9-18. Happy hour 6-8pm daily with 50% off all drinks. **Prices** Cocktails €12 , €5-8 for glasses of wine, beers €6-10, specialty drinks €10-12. **Web Site** www.restaurant-toi.com **Dress** Smart Casual…stylish. **Hot Nights/When to Go** Happy hour for a nice dinner or just half-priced drinks. Also, on the weekend around 11pm.

Tip from Brittney: "I want to meet this bar's interior decorator! It's super trendy, colorful, and fun inside this place, and you should come for happy hour to enjoy half-priced cocktails."

LATIN QUARTER

Bar du Marche

| Bar | 75 R. de Seine | Night |
| Daily 8am-2am | | |

3 2 3 3

The Scene A very lively Parisian bar with plenty of tables outside to escape the mayhem inside. This place gets packed on the weekends with locals looking to enjoy a crazy yet somehow civilized social scene. The bartenders/servers sport overalls and berets as they tend to the needs of their stylish and suave customers. Dim orange lights make for a lounge feel inside, while the outdoor tables attract a young-professional crowd. Everyone here looks good, seems friendly, and emits an upscale yet hip vibe, all at the same time. **Crowd** Slightly older crowd…late 20s to 40s…well-dressed yet casual…. a mixture of young professionals and trendy liberals. **Entertainment/Music** Loud conversation is the music here (sometimes soft French music in the background). **Prices** Beers €3-4, coffee €2, cocktails/wine €5 and up. **Dress** Casual but stylish. **Hot Nights/When to Go** F/Sa around 11pm.

Tip from Brittney: "I like the feel of this place. It's so French, and I like meeting the older, successful guys who aren't afraid to buy an American girl some vino. Come here around 11pm for a great opportunity to meet some Parisians."

Bob Cool

| Bar | 15 R.des Grands Augustins | Night |
| Daily 5pm-2am | | |

2 3 2 3

The Scene A most friendly little Parisian bar with great Happy hour specials and a cozy atmosphere. Bob Cool has an artsy feel with a huge mural on the wall of cartoon characters enjoying a drink, playing music, or engaged in other frivolity. Come here for cocktails and meet people from all over the world. While the front of the bar is bright and very colorful, the back is dark, with stone walls, but still quite inviting. It is, as the name implies, cool. **Crowd** This place prides itself on having the friendliest crowd of any bar. They draw and interesting mix of French, English, and Americans from ages 18 to 55. No matter what their age, patrons here stay casual as they wind down after a long day. **Entertainment/Music** No particular musical style. They like to change it up, but lots of Drum and Bass or chill techno. **Food/Misc** No food here. **Prices** Happy hour from 5-9pm for 2 for 1 cocktails, pints for €4, and half pints for €2. Cocktails are €7.50 normally, and beers are €6 for a pint, €4 for a half- pint. **Dress** Casual. **Hot Nights/When to Go** Happy Hour on the weekends for the drink deals and the crowd.

Tip from Emma: "On a Friday afternoon, this is a great place to come for Happy hour. The crowd is so friendly, and no one is too shy to start a conversation with you. Very welcoming spot."

Boulevard St-Michel	Square		**Night**
and Environs	All Day and Night		Day

[3] [3] [3] [3]

PARIS LATIN QUARTER

The Scene So, you have finally seen that famous cathedral Notre Dame. It is beautiful, but now take time to meet people and grab some drinks in the more upscale part of the Latin Quarter, around Blvd St. Michel. Although it is called the Latin Quarter, this area has flavors from all over world. Chinese, Greeks, Japanese, and the French all contribute to make this section of Paris lively and fun. Narrow cobblestone streets, great for wandering aimlessly, are lined with tons of bars, restaurants, and shops filled with souvenirs. At all times of day, something is going on here, and you may even hear some free music from street performers. The actual Blvd St. Michel is a large street with recognizable store names, but it is worth your while to take some time to stray from the main area to get a more European taste. **Crowd** By day, this area is full of tourists from all over and lots of Americans. At night, however, the French come here to meet friends and party until late in the night. Some bars and restaurants are a little dressy, but a casual look will be fine. **Entertainment/Music** Sometimes at night, you will hear a man belting out opera-like tunes while you sit and eat. Technically, it is free, but you should tip him. **Food/Misc** Restaurants serve cuisine from all over. Lots of Greek, Italian, and, of course, French. **Dress** Casual. **Hot Nights/When to Go** Weekends are busiest, but you'll find a good crowd anytime. **Close By** With so many places to go, it may be hard to decide where to pop in for a drink. *Le Lutece* is right in the Blvd. and allows you to sit outside and do all the people watching you want. Inside the little village-like area is an upscale cocktail bar called the *Latin Corner*, which is a place for women (due to the stripping male waiters).

Tip from Adam: "It can be a bit tiring just waking around here, so just find a place to relax. After walking the narrow streets, grab a bottle of wine and enjoy the sights on the sidewalk along the Seine."

Café Mabillon

Bar	164 Blvd. St. German	**Night**
Daily 7am-6am		

PARIS LATIN QUARTER

👤 **3** 👤 **2** 👤 **4** 👤 **1**

The Scene A very upscale bar with seating right on the street, and it's open 23 hours a day (one hour closed to clean). The mood is set by the dim red lighting, stained-glass art, modern furniture, and a candle to illuminate every table. A very chill place to hang out, especially at a table on the sidewalk. This is a really fun place to hit with your friends to enjoy one of the hundreds of cocktails. However, since you are sitting at a small table with friends, it's somewhat hard to meet people here.
Crowd Frequented by an older crowd in their 30s to 40s dressed in nice clothes. Perhaps they are coming here from work. **Food/Misc** They cook up tasty sandwiches, as well as bigger meals like ravioli and traditional French cuisine. **Prices** No cover charge, but drinks can be expensive. Cocktails start at €11. **Dress** Smart casual. **Hot Nights/When to Go** The biggest crowd gathers on the weekends, but you can have a good time here any night of the week. Stays crowded late.

Tip from Brittney: "This is a place you want to come with friends to splurge a little and sit outside. Order a couple of cocktails before moving to your next place. Even come back late night if you feel like it."

The 5th Bar

Bar	62 R. Mouffetard	**Night**
Su-Th 4pm-2am, F-Sa 4pm-4am		

👤 **3** 👤 **2** 👤 **0** 👤 **2**

The Scene Located in the Latin Quarter is a tiny place that has a little bit of everything for the Anglos. The epitome of eclectic décor, The 5th Bar sports Halloween decorations in June and walls plastered with anything from fine art to beer posters. The basement atmosphere is like that of a dungeon with a skeleton shrine. The vibe here eludes definition, but they offer lots of extras that may attract you. **Crowd** Lots of Anglos hit this bar, so the language barrier is not a problem. Let loose here and leave your nice clothes at the hotel for another night.
Entertainment/Music The bartender is the DJ, and she plays any kind of music. The genre can change from one song to the next.
Food/Misc Tu: happy hour until 10pm. W: all shots are €2.50. Th: Happy hour lasts all night and is Alabama Slammer night. Su: they show The Simpsons from 7-9pm and at 9pm NFL Football, when in season. **Prices** Weekdays until 6pm: pint blonds for €3.50. Normally, drinks from €5-8. **Dress** Casual. **Hot Nights/When to Go** Thursday nights are most crowded.

Tip from Tuck: "This place may be a little different, but if they have NFL football, I am definitely going."

Frog and Princess Pub

Pub	9 R. Princesse	**Night**
Daily 12pm-2am		Day

👤 4　👤 3　👤 1　👤 4

PARIS:LATIN QUARTER

The Scene This French pub, a sports bar that brews its own beer, has a feel unlike other Parisian bars. Without the frills of some other venues, you are free to focus on beer and sports. Large kegs are connected directly to their taps for a wide variety of the freshest beer around. A great place to enjoy sporting events, since it offers as many TVs are any bar we've seen in Paris. It may be no match for your favorite sports bar in the States, but you'll feel right at home with the friendly crowd and have a good time nonetheless. **Crowd** Tuesday night is student night here, so the crowd is primarily…students. Hence, folks are casual and friendly. You can even scream at the game on TV and not feel out of place. Frog and Princess draws and international crowd and lots of English-speakers. **Entertainment/Music** Lots of sports on TV. **Food/Misc** Typical bar food served everyday from 5:30 until 11:30pm, and brunch served Saturday and Sunday from 12-4pm. The have bar snacks (wings, nachos with cheese, potato skins, etc.), hamburgers, and salads. Sunday is quiz night. They also have a frequent drinker program, so ask for a card and earn enough stamps for a free jug. The cards work at any Frog and Princess in Europe. **Prices** Pint of beer starts at €6, jugs start at €20. Student night prices are €4.50 for beers and some cocktails. **Web Site** www.frogpubs.com, princess@frog-pubs.com **Dress** Casual. **Hot Nights/When to Go** Tuesday night is student night. Also fun during any big sporting event.

Tip from Emma: "This is fun place to come to anytime, but if you are on a budget, Tuesday nights will save you some money. Great time to come and meet other students; just make sure to bring your student card in case they ask."

Latin Corner Café

Bar	27 R. de la Huchette	**Night**
Daily until 4am		

👤 0　👤 0　👤 4　👤 2

The Scene This upscale bar has a loungy feel, even by day, with a heavy techno beat in the background and a warm glow created by orange, red, and yellow flashing lights. There is, however, a twist…after 9pm, they stop allowing all guys into the bar, because it transforms into a Strip Tease joint for girls. Latin waiters dance from table to table in little shorts and tight black tank tops entertaining the women with strip teases. A great spot for a fun and different (for sure!) girls' night out. **Crowd** What you won't find here are men, except for the waiters. The girls that come here are young and beautiful. They love to get dressed up to hit this spot. **Entertainment/Music** DJ here plays techno music to which the waiters dance. **Food/Misc** Strip Teases. **Prices** Happy hour 4-9pm: cocktails €6, normally €10. **Dress** Smart casual. **Hot Nights/When to Go** If you are a girl, go after 9pm. Guys, however, should come before then to enjoy the many cute girls having drinks for happy hour.

Tip from Brittney: "A nice cocktail bar with entertainment to boot. It's kind of fun to check out the provocative dancing, and I suggest giving your waiter a tip."

Le 10 Bar	Bar	10 R. de l'Odeon	**Night**
	Daily 5:30pm-2am		

The Scene Take a step back in time into an old Parisian bar in which patrons converse about worldly matters over a class of sangria. With posters and paintings portraying what Paris once was and a bartender likely to belt out tunes over the light French music, this smoky little bar is a nice break from spots on the main streets. Le 10 Bar offers a ton of character in a unique setting - enjoy it. **Crowd** Students like to come here to drink Sangria, the house specialty, smoke cigarettes, and converse about life, love, and the world. It draws a nice mixture of French and Americans. **Entertainment/Music** Old French music plays lightly in the background, and there is jukebox that works sometimes. **Prices** Sangria €3, beers and mixed drinks €3-4. **Dress** Casual. **Hot Nights/When to Go** It draws a crowd every night around 9pm, but on the weekends it gets even busier.

Tip from Emma: "For such a tiny bar, this place has a ton of character. When you come here, make sure to order the sangria and ask the bartender to sing for you. A great place to meet other intellectuals."

Le Violin Dingue	Bar	46 R. de la Montagne Ste.	**Night**
	Weekdays 6pm-1:30am, weekends 6pm-3:30am		

The Scene A place to meet people for sure, Violin Dingue is super-friendly towards Americans who have made their way to Paris. The upstairs feels like any typical bar, but the downstairs is a unique place to hang out. They call it the cave, and it feels like one as you descend into it. The patrons here create a lively atmosphere and make this a bar worth coming to. As the night goes on, the crowd becomes even friendlier. Want to dance? No one here will turn you down. Take a break from the French here; it is well worth the trip. **Crowd** Lots of young people, the majority of whom are students or just out of college. It seems that everyone at the bar speaks English. The energetic and friendly crowd loves to have fun all night and to avoid cheesy Parisian clubs. **Entertainment/Music** American Rock, because who adds the roll anymore. **Food/Misc** Sign out front says they accept US dollars. **Prices** Happy hour from 8-10pm for €3-4 pints and bottled beers for €2-3, cocktails are €4.50, shots are €2.50. To enter the cave downstairs, the Cover charge is €10 for guys and free for girls. Regular pints start at €6, mixed drinks for €7. **Hot Nights/When to Go** Any night of the week, this place attracts a crowd, but the weekends are the most fun.

Tip from Adam: "Even if your game is in shambles, it is impossible not to strike up a conversation with a cute American girl."

Le Who's Bar

Bar	13 R. du Petit Pont	**Night**
Daily 6pm-6am		

The Scene This bar can be a little pricey if you don't stop by during happy hour (8-10pm), but it is worth it if there is live music. Mirrors cover the walls, and a slightly older crowd congregates here for great mixed drinks and socializing. The space is small, but when it gets really packed, they open up a downstairs room. The music varies by the night but is always loud and sets the tone for a lively atmosphere. Very dim lighting adds to the intimacy here, and Le Who's is a great casual environment in which to chill out with some friends. **Crowd** Late 20s to late 40s donning casual bar attire...seems to be more locals than tourists, which creates a true Parisian feel. **Entertainment/Music** Randomly, they offer live music. **Food/Misc** Reduced prices between 8-10pm nightly for happy hour. **Prices** Beers are €5 for a small and €9 for a large, cocktails are €11-12. **Dress** Casual. **Hot Nights/When to Go** 8-10pm nightly for happy hour specials and when there is live music.

Tip from Adam: "Come by for happy hour after grabbing dinner at a Brasserie in the area. The loud, eclectic music really helps get you goin' for the night."

Luxembourg Gardens

Outdoor activity		
Daytime		Day

The Scene Set behind the Palace du Luxembourg is a beautiful park comprised of lovely gardens full of people out to enjoy a nice day. Gravel paths on which to walk or hang out weave throughout the gardens. Although there are many beautiful green lawns, only certain ones are available for public use, and most visitors are resting on the chairs they provide. The focal point of the gardens is a pond where children gather to play with ducks and race toy boats (which can be rented). Grab a picnic lunch and a bottle of wine and spend the afternoon here. You'll enjoy the buzz of laughter, happy chatter, and, occasionally, some live music. **Crowd** Tourists and locals alike come here to enjoy the scenery. Visitors' ages range from very young to very old. Lots of families, couples, and groups of friends. **Entertainment/Music** At any time, there could be some kind of musical performance, but it is best to get away from that and enjoy some peace and quiet. **Food/Misc** Small stands located around the gardens sell hot dogs, sandwiches, ice cream, and drinks. **Prices** No price for admission. Toy boat rental €1.80 for 30 minutes, and €3 for 1 hour. **Dress** Casual. **Hot Nights/When to Go** On a nice, sunny day **Close By** Located just outside of the gardens are plenty of French brassieres with outdoor seating. These particular spots tend to have a little bit of an older crowd, but if you walk for approximately 10 minutes down Rue de Tournon until you come to Blvd. St. Germain, you will find more young bars and hang outs like the *Frog and Princess Pub* and *Café Mabillion*.

Tip from Adam: "Come chill in gardens on a nice day and find a grassy spot to take in the scene. Bring along some beers and food and enjoy the peace and quiet of these gardens."

March Monge

	Other	Monge metro	
	W, F, Su 8am-1:30pm		Day

 3 3 3 4

The Scene On Wednesday, Friday, and Sunday mornings and into the early afternoons, the square located above the Place Monge metro becomes an open-air market where all kinds of people bring their goods to be sold. Fresh fruits, vegetables, breads, meats, and cheeses are abundant. Basically, any kind of food you can think of and even some clothing lines the square. Markets always provide a great way to meet locals and get a flavor of the culture. Spend some time here taking in the sights and smells; grab some food and set up a picnic. **Crowd** A variety of people enjoy this market. Many locals do their grocery shopping here, and tourists are everywhere just checking out the scene. **Dress** Anything goes. **Close By** Around the square are little cafes and brassieres. *The Buffet Chard et Freud* has friendly service and pinball. *Le Monge Tabac* is another brassiere at which to grab a drink and a smoke. *Au Rendezvous du Marche* is a small neighborhood bar with a pool table and off-track horse betting.

Tip from Emma: "Come for a little cultural flavor of the Latin Quarter. Find some food that appeals to you and a spot to eat. In between Marche Monge and rue Mouffetard is a tiny park with some shade."

Polly McGoo's

	Bar	3 et 5 R. du Petit Pont	**Night**
	Daily 9am - 2am		

 2 3 2 3

The Scene Polly McGoo's is covered with tiles in the unique style of Antonio Gaudi, Barcelona's most famous artist. Wrought iron railings and detailed tile designs define the décor in this bohemian bar. There is an authentically friendly feel here with a bit of Spanish flair to liven things up. Head upstairs, if you're with a crowd, to catch some live music or mingle downstairs to meet people of all ages and backgrounds by the long, wraparound bar. Polly McGoo's is just a feel-good spot to enjoy some cocktails away from the typical French-style bars. The friendly clientele and laid-back atmosphere are welcoming. **Crowd** A young crowd of friendly and inviting patrons…mostly 20s to mid 30s…casual. **Entertainment/Music** Live music upstairs, occasionally (small groups or a man with a guitar and a microphone). **Food/Misc** Appetizers €3-10, pizza €8-10, other Spanish entrees €12-15. **Prices** Cocktails €5-8, beers €3-5. **Dress** Casual. **Hot Nights/When to Go** Gets packed around 10pm, especially on the weekends.

Tip from Emma: "If you enjoy meeting friendly people, be sure to stop by Polly McGoo's for a night. The entire Saint Michel area is a lot of fun, and this place has such a lively Spanish flavor to mix things up."

River Bar

	Pub/Café	40 R. Descartes	**Night**
	Daily until 2am		

PARIS LATIN QUARTER

👤 2 👤 3 👤 2 👤 3

The Scene The River Bar is a great, small pub for meeting up with friends in the Latin Quarter. It's trendy with Indian artwork on the walls and dim Victorian-style lights. You may notice some Spanish flair here, and if you happen to pick the right night, you may even catch some live music. Everyone here is extremely friendly, laid back, and casual. This place really gives off a 'small-town' feel, and there are plenty of cozy seats/tables in the back for relaxing. **Crowd** A young, college-aged crowd…early 20s to 30s…a little on the artsy and trendy side in terms of dress/style. **Entertainment/Music** Live music occasionally…otherwise, trendy, modern beats. **Food/Misc** Happy Hour reduced drink price specials. **Prices** Beers €2-4.50 during Happy hour and €3-6 otherwise, cocktails (long island iced teas, sex on the beach, etc.) about €6, flavored vodka shots all night long for €2. **Dress** Completely casual. **Hot Nights/When to Go** Like most of the Latin Quarter, this place is a little quieter during the summer, because students aren't around. Nonetheless, Tuesdays and Fridays happen to be the best nights, around 10pm.

Tip from Emma: "I love how casual and down to earth everyone is here. You'll feel the Spanish influence in this great little pub, and I recommend taking advantage of the €2 shots all night long."

Rue Mouffetard

	Square	R. Mouffetard	**Night**
	Anytime		Day

👤 3 👤 4 👤 3 👤 4

The Scene A students' scene that is fantastic for people-watching and the perfect place to catch the feel and spirit of the Latin Quarter, this street is full of cafes, bars, and small specialty shops. You'll find unique trinkets, funky jewelry, books for the intellectuals, and clothing for those who can't afford to shop on the Champs. Rue Mouffetard is like being in a quaint old village where there is no Superstore to meet all of your needs. Instead, there are the liquor stores, bakeries, cheese shops, fish market, fresh fruit stands, the butcher, and the candy makers - each specializing in one particular thing at which they happen to be very good. The atmosphere is casual and welcoming. **Crowd** Lots of students hang out around here, because the area is cheaper. However, people of all ages come to spend a day and meet all of their shopping needs. Locals here make you feel like part of their neighborhood. **Dress** Casual. **Hot Nights/When to Go** During the day or at night, there are people here to meet. **Close By** The street here is lined with bars and restaurants, but one thing you should look for is the bowling alley. They have cheap drinks, sangria for €3, and a rock and bowl feel. Although it is geared towards kids during the day, it can be fun thing to do early at night. Cost €3.50 for students from 7pm-2am. *The 5th Bar* and *River Bar* are also located on this street.

Tip from Emma: "You needn't drop any cash to check out the student social life in the Latin Quarter. Wander around and get the true feel for this area. Feels like being on main street in your college town. At the end of the street is a little fountain. On a hot day, sit on the edge and let the mist cool you off."

Shywawa

Bar	7 R. du Petit Pont	**Night**
Su-Th 5pm-5am, F-Sa 5pm-6am		

👨 3   👩 3   👩 1   👩 2

PARIS LATIN QUARTER

The Scene This dark and narrow little Irish pub is "dressed up" a bit with flashing holiday lights and funky bar stools that look like modern art. The back area offers a spot to gather with friends old and new and chat about life or play cards. Murals of vintage Parisian advertisements contribute to the funky décor. A casual spot to hear some good music.
Crowd A bit of an older crowd in their late 20s and 30s. They are very friendly here and not trying to look so fancy while they party.
Entertainment/Music They mix it up here from reggae to almost anything you want to hear. **Prices** Daily Happy hour until 9pm: €2 off of all cocktails and beers at reduced prices. Normally, pints start at €5.20, cocktails start at €6.50. **Dress** Casual. **Hot Nights/When to Go** If you are looking to meet people, it is best to come on a Friday or Saturday night. Most crowded time is 10pm-12:30am and again at 1:30am, especially on the weekends.

Tip from Adam: "What I like about this place is that they play a good mix of music, and you don't have to get dressed up to come here, even though it is in a nice area."

Young and Happy Hostel

Accomodation	80 R. Mouffetard	**Night**
Curfew 2am		

👨 3   👩 3   👩 2   👩 4

The Scene A quaint little hostel that is located in the heart of the Latin Quarter, the Young and Happy Hostel is full of young travelers looking to meet people and have a good time. They have two areas in which to hang out and do some partying before going out or when you come back. A tiny bar upstairs serves beer and wine, and visitors also hang out in the kitchen downstairs, which is quite cozy. A clean, bright, and genial hostel with a lively atmosphere. Be sure to call ahead - this place is tiny and fills up quickly. **Crowd** Young travelers from all over the world come here to stay. These are just the kinds of people you would expect to find staying at a hostel. **Food/Misc** They have a kitchen where you can cook your own food, but they don't have food for you. Although they serve alcohol, no outside alcohol is allowed in the hostel. This spot offers internet access, currency exchange without a commission, and an English speaking staff. **Prices** Singles for €20, doubles €23, sheet rental €2.50, and towel rental €1. Wine starts at €6.50, bottled beers start at €2.70. **Web Site** www.youngandhappy.fr **Dress** PJs. **Close By** The Latin Quarter! There are plenty of bars within easy walking distance. Some fun ones include the *5th Bar* and *River Bar*.

Tip from Emma: "This hostel is located in a great area with tons of student bars and little boutiques. The place is clean and, because it is small, it is really easy to meet other people. Just beware of the curfew, because they can be really strict about this."

MARAIS

Chez Richard

Lounge	37 R. Vieille-du-Temple	**Night**
Daily 6pm-2am		

👤 3   👤 2   👤 4   👤 2

The Scene During the day, a little bit of natural light comes in from the skylight over the bar, but at night the place stays dark and warm. A beautiful lounge in which the downstairs bar is an incredible mosaic of blues, greens, and reds, reminiscent of Barcelona. Modern steel sculptures contribute to the classy décor and refined ambiance. So nice, it's like being at an exclusive club without the exclusivity. **Crowd** A bit of an older and sophisticated crowd, but they are welcoming. The patrons here look well dressed and fashionable; so, avoid your cheap backpacking garb. **Entertainment/Music** On the weekends, there is a DJ. Although they claim to play a wide variety of music, you will most often hear techno creating a lounge mood. **Food/Misc** A small restaurant upstairs serves very good French cuisine. **Prices** Cocktails start at €8.60, glasses of wine start at €3.80. **Dress** Dressy club-attire. **Hot Nights/When to Go** Saturday night draws the best crowd. Arrive early enough to get a table.

Tip from Brittney: "My favorite area to hang out in here is on the couches downstairs by the mosaic bar. Grab a cocktail, enjoy the gorgeous interior, and people-watch on a crowded Saturday night."

Les Petits Marseillais

Restaurant	72 R. Vieille du Temple	**Night**
Daily until 2am		

👤 3   👤 3   👤 4   👤 2

The Scene This is nothing less than an incredible, quaint, local restaurant that you should try for a delicious dinner. Located in a very trendy neighborhood on a small side street, Les Petits Marseillais is known for its amazing seafood entrees, romantic atmosphere, and eclectic menu. It is as Parisian as can be, so don't expect to see any English on the menu or many tourists dining here. A tranquil ambiance is created by a very dark interior with candles everywhere and beautiful waitresses. This is a place you need to try for a truly authentic French wining and dining experience. **Crowd** Attracts a very hip, trendy Parisian crowd in their late 20s to 40s. **Entertainment/Music** Great, modern, melodic, and soothing music to relax you as you dine. **Food/Misc** Seafood, beef, pastas, specialty salads, cous cous, homemade tarts, amazing French cuisine…starters €6-10, main dishes €12-20, bottles of wine starting at €19. **Prices** Drinks are appropriately priced, beers for €4-7, cocktails €7-8, etc. **Dress** Smart Casual…stylish, swanky. **Hot Nights/When to Go** Great weekend dining experience, but good any night of the week.

Tip from Brittney: "This is a must do place on a Sunday evening or any night you're looking to regroup from a lot of partying and splurge on a fantastic meal. This is the cutest little French restaurant and an amazing place to escape the tourist scene with some friends."

Lizard Lounge	Bar	18 R. du Bourg-Tibourg	**Night**
	Daily 12pm-2am, Happy Hour 6pm-10pm		

The Scene An in vogue place for young people, Lizard Lounge offers a fresh feel and a modern attitude. The bar, with the feel of a lounge, does not look too big until you work your way downstairs; this is where you want to be. Dim red lighting throughout creates a chill atmosphere that is enhanced by a low stone ceiling. Making your way around the underground, as it is appropriately called, feels like navigating a network of caves. The DJ in the underground sets the tone, which makes you want either to lounge or to dance. Either way, it is sure to be a good time. **Crowd** A polished, casual look is the trend among this International crowd with plenty of English speakers. **Entertainment/Music** They have a DJ from Wednesday-Sunday until closing, and sometimes they offer live music. The music is sometimes jazz, but mainly techno leaning toward drum and bass. **Food/Misc** Chips and salsa, guacamole, burgers, and salads. **Prices** Happy hour every day from 8-10pm: all cocktails and pints are €4.60. Otherwise, pints start at €6.20, food ranges from €5-12. **Web Site** www.cheapblonde.com **Dress** Smart casual. **Hot Nights/When to Go** Happy hour and the weekends, but anytime they have live music, the crowd gets bigger.

Tip from Brittney: "The lounge area in the underground is a great place to hang out. Meet some people here or bring friends down with you and get lost in the caves. I love to come for Happy hour."

Petit Fer a Cheval	Wine Bar	30, R. Vieille-du-Temple	**Night**
	Daily 9am-2am		Day

The Scene This tiny bar/restaurant sports décor reminiscent of a French palace of yesteryear. The bar is made of fine engraved wood topped with elegant marble. From above, an intricate golden chandelier hangs to illuminate a cozy bar perfectly fit for conversation. In fact, this unique u-shaped bar is so small that it is possible to talk with someone sitting on the other side of it. This is an intimate and hospitable place to come sip wine or beer on a nice summer's evening. **Crowd** The crowd generally ranges from 21-35, but it can get older. The bar is nice, so the patrons tend to be somewhat sophisticated and a little better dressed. They draw a mix of French, Americans, and others nationalities as well. The people here are friendly and interested in having a good time. **Entertainment/Music** You won't find a focus on music here. Petit Fer a Cheval is more about the lively and very intimate atmosphere created by its patrons. **Food/Misc** French cuisine. They serve food until 1am (occasionally until 1:30am). **Prices** Beers start at €4.50, cocktails start at €7.50, €1 charge to sit outside, entrees start about €11, appetizers for approximately €4. **Dress** Smart casual. **Hot Nights/When to Go** The weekends get the most crowded, but it is fun here any night, especially around 8 or 9pm to start out the night.

Tip from Emma: "I have never seen a bar like this one. It so small that you can talk to someone on the other side of it...great for conversation. Come here around 8 or 9pm for a drink or two then move on. You will definitely want a place at the bar so you don't have to pay the extra money."

Stolly's

Bar	16 R. Cloche Perce	Night
Daily 4pm - 2am		

👤 3 👤 3 👤 1 👤 2

The Scene Although it may be a bit hard to find tucked away in a corner, this cheap blonde bar is worth it. A great place for English speakers to hang out and feel a little more at home among other friendly folks who seem to be escaping Paris. The inside space is small, but an outside patio provides a nice reprieve from Paris' harried pace on a nice day. The décor is random - sporting a bear statue, a lava lamp, and a Roy Liechtenstein print - but unimportant, for the real ambiance here is created by the patrons. Come here to listen to American music and chat with other Anglos at this friendly, neighborhood-style bar.
Crowd The crowd is young, mostly English-speaking, and completely laid back; don't get dressed up. **Entertainment/Music** They play American rock music here (but not hip-hop). **Prices** Happy hour 4:30-8pm for reduced drink prices. Cheap Blonde, the bar's specialty, is only €5 a pint and €13 for a jug, bottled beers start at €3.90, kamikaze shots are €5. **Web Site** www.cheapblonde.com **Dress** Casual.
Hot Nights/When to Go The bar is most crowded on the weekends. Come around 11pm for the biggest crowds.

Tip from Tuck: "Having problems ordering a beer in French? Come to Stolly's. They will understand you without a problem. On a nice day, get some fresh air outside, because the inside gets a little stuffy."

Villa Keops

Bar	58 Blvd. Sebastopol	Night
M-Th 12pm-2am, F-Sa 12pm-4am, Su 4pm-3am		

👤 2 👤 2 👤 3 👤 2

The Scene This is a swanky place loaded with modern and trendy decor. Vibrant colors, funky seats, and a fancy food and drink menu are just a piece of the atmosphere here. Funky, techno-style music is always pumping as patrons sip their Mojitos. Tables are illuminated with candles to contribute to Villa Keops' exceptionally romantic feel.
Crowd A very stylish and eclectic crew in their mid-20s to mid-30s.
Entertainment/Music Hip, groovy, melodic techno or house music.
Food/Misc Starters €11-12, main dishes (meats and fish, upscale sandwiches, salads, etc.) €12-14. Reduced prices during happy hour 7-9pm. **Prices** Vino €6, cocktails €8.5, shots €6.5, beers €3.50-5.50.
Dress Smart Casual. **Hot Nights/When to Go** Weekends during happy hour (7pm-9pm).

Tip from Brittney: "This is another great Happy hour bar with amazing cocktails. I would only head here with a crowd."

PARISMARAIS

MONTMARTRE

Chez Camille

Bar	8 R. Ravignan	**Night**
M-W 5pm-2am, Sa-Su 2pm-2am		Day

| 3 | 4 | 2 | 4 |

The Scene Soft, slow techno brings you in sync with this super-trendy hole-in-the-wall bar. This is a joint the locals love to take advantage of and bask in its artsy intimacy. Drinks are cheap, and everyone here is as friendly as you're gonna find in Paris. This is a great place to unwind over some cocktails and a smoke, especially on a beautiful afternoon. Make sure to drop by Chez Camille at some point to experience that "home away from home" feel in a true Parisian environment. **Crowd** An artsy, liberal, and trendy crowd in their mid-20s and up, these folks are super-friendly and laid back. **Entertainment/Music** Varies, but usually modern, melodic techno that actually mellows you out.
Food/Misc Small bar snacks at best. **Prices** Shots €2.80, beers €3.5, mixed drinks €6, glasses of wine €3.5. **Dress** Completely casual.
Hot Nights/When to Go Saturday and Sunday all day long.

Tip from Adam: "You gotta let yourself marinate at this place at least one night or afternoon while in Paris. Smoke a little, chill out, and bullshit with some of the locals at Chez Camille…there are some extremely fascinating characters here."

Corcoran's Irish Pub

Pub/Café	110 Blvd. de Clichy	**Night**
M-W until 4am, Th 4.30am, F/Sa 5am, Su 4am		Day

| 3 | 3 | 2 | 3 |

The Scene This traditional (but huge) Irish pub is loaded with Guinness paraphernalia and other typical Irish décor. A huge outdoor awning provides cover to a multitude of tables on the sidewalk, and inside, you can enjoy tons of big TVs showing a variety of sporting events. There is a long bar that almost runs the length of the pub itself, and in the back, you'll find a pool table, booths, and a more intimate setting great for conversation. This pub serves a variety of food and is open until the early morning hours for the true Anglo-Saxon drinkers.
Crowd Lots of English speaking folks in their mid-20s to 40s…casually dressed but with a preppy bent…very social and inviting.
Entertainment/Music Pool table, TVs, photohunt. **Food/Misc** Food served 11am-11pm M-F and 11am-9:30pm Sa and Su (Irish stew, hamburgers, fish n chips, etc.) for €9-11, snacks €4-8, Irish breakfast €13 on the weekends. Happy hour 5-8pm daily with reduced prices on all drinks. **Prices** Beers €3-6, Cocktails €7.50. **Dress** Casual.
Hot Nights/When to Go Hit it either for a meal and Happy hour cocktails any day or on the weekends around 11:30pm.

Tip from Tuck: "If you enjoy the friendly atmosphere of traditional Irish pubs, then you'll love this massive one. Corcoran's is quite big but still very authentic and loaded with great Irish/English drinkers. Come here for some fish 'n chips during Happy hour and grab a few pints."

La Fourmi

Bar	74 R. des Martyrs	**Night**
M-Th 8am-2am, F-Sa 8am-4am, Su 10am-2am		Day

PARISMONTMARTRE

3 3 2 3

The Scene This place draws its eclectic crowd from the surrounding area. Very much a local scene here with a variety of artists and music-lovers gathering for drinks. La Fourmi has a very friendly, low-key, and relaxed atmosphere all day and all night long. There is nothing commercial about this joint, and its industrial interior sets the hip mood. The neighborhood in which La Fourmi is located happens to host a good number of local concerts, so this place serves as a fantastic pre/post-show watering hole. **Crowd** A local crowd here in their early 20s to late 30s with a very casual and hippy style about them; loaded with liberal and artsy folk. **Entertainment/Music** Light hip-hop on the weekends, though it can vary depending on the night. **Food/Misc** Full menu all day and night - typical French cuisine including meat, fries, crepes, etc. **Prices** Beers €4-7, Food €5-15, Coffee €2-4.
Dress Completely casual. **Hot Nights/When to Go** Whenever the local music venues are hosting local bands.

Tip from Adam: "Talk to some locals about when good shows are playing in the area. Hit up La Fourmi for some coffee/drinks before and after the show, and you'll be sure to meet some fellow chill hippies."

Le Village Hostel

Accomodation	20 R. d'Orsel	**Night**
Curfew 2am		Day

3 2 2 3

The Scene Look no further for extremely nice/clean living conditions at a great price. Although it is not a rowdy party hostel, Le Village Hostel does offer excellent proximity to the bustling Montmartre area. With the Sacre Coeur practically right next door and an array of restaurants, bars, and shops surrounding it, this is a nice option for young backpackers. They do sell beer inside the hostel, though they don't allow you to bring in your own alcohol. The staff speaks English quite well, and you may enjoy the friendly, somewhat calm atmosphere maintained here.
Crowd Attracts a variety of travelers from all over the world...mostly young (20s) backpackers and vacationers. **Entertainment/Music** Kitchen facilities, shower and toilet in every room, telephone/fax, internet available. **Food/Misc** Breakfast is included in the price of every room.
Prices March-October: Dorm (4 to 6 beds) €23, Triple €25, Double/Twin €27. Off-season: Dorm €20, Triple €21.50, Double/Twin €23. Sheets €2.50, Towels €1. All prices are per person.
Web Site www.villagehostel.fr. **Close By** Metro, post office, supermarkets, bakeries, restaurants, clubs. Check out the review of Sacre Coeur for more details on places nearby…great location.

Tip from Emma: "This is one of the nicest hostels I've seen, and you may like the fact that it is a little quieter than some of the party hostels. It is a great place to come for friendly and clean accommodations, and all the partying you need is either nearby or just a metro ride away."

Sacre Coeur

	Other	Anvers metro stop	
		Day	

PARISMONTMARTRE

3 3 3 4

The Scene Stroll onto rue du Stinkerque off of Blvd Rochechouart and head up the cobblestone street towards the Cathedral Sacre Coeur. The scene here is diverse and entertaining. You'll find yourself immediately surrounded by tons of little cafes, brasseries, and shops selling soccer jerseys and artwork of Paris, etc. At the base of Sacre Coeur is a little merry-go-round for children, and you can catch the view by either taking the Funiculaire (which is to your left and costs €2.50) or just walking up the stairs to the top. The lawn on the way to the top is loaded with sunbathers and people of all ages relaxing on the grass. About 3/4 of the way up is a viewing deck with binoculars (€2) providing a full and magnificent view of the city. It's really quite spectacular and even better when you get to the top. Be sure to take a look inside this world-renowned, breathtaking cathedral, and enjoy the music and acts of the local street performers outside. The area surrounding Sacre Coeur has so much to offer, so allow some time for wandering aimlessly. **Crowd** All ages and all types of people congregate here…locals and tourists alike. **Prices** Funiculaire costs €2.5 for a ride to the top. **Close By** For €5, you can jump on the ***Petit Train de Montmarte***, just to the left of Sacre Coeur, for a 35-minute tour around the entire hillside. This little train on wheels lets you take in all the sights of Montmarte at a very reasonable price. You can also head to the left of Sacre Coeur up rue Saint Eleuthere on foot and find wonderful little side streets, home to amazing artists working right before your eyes, cafes, musicians, etc. Pop into ***Claron de Chasseurs*** for crepes, coffee, pizza, live jazz…you name it. Another restaurant that's sure to be packed and will provide a great view of the street "events" is ***La Boheme***. This entire area really deserves some attention after you've enjoyed the Cathedral for a while.

Tip from Emma: "Sacre Coeur is the heart of the Montmarte region of Paris, and it is absolutely spectacular. You can spend hours around this place, and all it might cost you is a cup of coffee at a local café. Don't be afraid to wander around up here…you never know what little shop, brasserie, or street performance you might wander into."

PIGALLE

Bus Palladium

Club	6 R. Fontaine	Night
	Tu-Sa 11pm-6am	

3   2   4   4

The Scene A place where the young, hip, and beautiful come to party. Guys, if you want to enjoy this place, bring some cash, but Tuesdays are completely free for the ladies. Although the décor is somewhat reminiscent of the 50s, it is too dark to take much notice of that. What you will notice is an area in which the purchase of a bottle enables you to hang out on posh red leather couches while beautiful and scantily clad women dance on tables. The ambiance is classy and sophisticated, and the past three generations seem to meld here. **Crowd** You are going to find a young crowd here with some money to spend. Patrons vary depending on the night, so expect anything. **Entertainment/Music** The music varies by night and can be hip-hop, rock, techno, or disco. Some nights you will hear a mix of everything. **Prices** Cover charge up to €20, all drinks €13, bottles of liquor for €160, which gives access to a private table and dance entertainment. Free cover and drinks for ladies on Tuesday. **Dress** Dressy club attire.
Hot Nights/When to Go Girls, go on Tuesday and drink for free all night. Not a bad deal.

Tip from Emma: "Check this hot spot out on Tuesday to save the huge cover and drink fees. Wear something nice to be let in quickly."

Folies Pigalle

Club	11 Pl. Pigalle	Night
	Su 5pm-6am, Tu-Th 12am-6am, F-Sa 12am-12pm	

1   0   3   1

The Scene This late night, crazed festival of trance and hardcore techno is nothing less than outrageous. Barraged by loud music, lights, and smoke, you will feel like you have entered another world, and the party goes on all night and well into the morning…no one seems to want it to end. Although the crowd is largely homosexual, all types come here for the frenetic party atmosphere. It is certainly easiest to meet those who are hanging out off the dance floor. This spot, one of the wildest in all of Paris, is not for the faint-hearted traveler. **Crowd** A primarily male crowd (many of whom are gay), but some girls do enjoy the scene. Patrons, in crazy attire, seem to have no trouble staying up all night dancing. **Entertainment/Music** The music here is trance and hardcore techno all night. **Prices** Cover charge €20 (includes 1 drink). **Dress** Anything goes here…the more outrageous the better.
Hot Nights/When to Go Friday and Saturday nights are the most crowded, and this is definitely a late night spot to hit after 2am.

Tip from Brittney: "This club is one of Paris' craziest and most entertaining to me. The crowd is truly not afraid to leave everything on the dance floor all night long. If you are feeling the urge to really blow it out, get here late and party all through the night and into the early morning."

O'Sullivans by the Mill

Pub/Café	92 Blvd du Clichy	**Night**
Daily 12pm-5am (until 6am F/Sa)		Day

👦 3   👧 2   👧 2   👧 3

The Scene Don't be fooled by the name; this isn't your traditional Irish pub. O'Sullivan's (the largest Anglo-Saxon bar in Paris) is a very modern, hip bar with enough of an Irish flair to stay true to its roots. This place is gigantic when they open up the back room during major sporting events or on Friday and Saturday nights. A huge L-shaped bar, plenty of comfortable chairs, and multiple big screen TVs offer plenty of enjoyment. Every Thursday, they get quality live bands in the back room, and the place really gets jumping. **Crowd** A crowd in their 20s and 30s; many Irish, English, and Australians here…preppy feel. **Entertainment/Music** Live music on Thursdays; rock and modern music otherwise, and TVs everywhere. **Food/Misc** Lunch: 12pm-7pm (sandwiches & light salads) €6-9; Dinner: 7pm-midnight (burgers, pastas, chicken) €10-12. **Prices** Pints €5-6, shots €5, mixed drinks €7-10. Cover charge €10 Friday and Saturday after 1am (includes a drink and use of coat check). €1 supplement for all drinks after 1am. **Web Site** www.osullivans-pubs.com **Dress** Casual…preppy. **Hot Nights/When to Go** On Thursdays, they have live bands on the stage in the beautiful backroom, so come by around 10 or 11pm.

Tip from Tuck: "It's so nice to be able to speak English with the girls here. On top of that, you can either hear a great U2 cover band or watch your favorite sporting events… all under one roof. Get here before 1am and dodge the cover"

Woodstock Hostel

Accomodation	48 R. Rodier	**Night**
Curfew 2am		

👦 3   👧 4   👧 3   👧 4

The Scene Woodstock Hostel is a great place for backpackers on a budget in Paris. It is a cozy and fun place to meet other travelers from around the world, and you'll definitely enjoy your stay here. As long as you can be in by 2am, you'll find that this place has everything you need and expect from a hostel. The funky atmosphere even features a Volkswagen beetle coming through one of the walls, an old foosball table, real hippie decor, and you can buy beers from the front desk. You'll hear some great stories and, hopefully, make some of your own to tell while staying here. **Crowd** Diverse, but mostly young, hip travelers looking to meet other interesting and fun backpackers. **Entertainment/Music** They play old American rock in the reception area…stuff from the Woodstock era like Janis Joplin. **Food/Misc** Breakfast included (from 8-9:30am), kitchen, English-speaking staff, baggage storage room, credit cards accepted, foreign currency exchanged, free maps, safety deposit box, fax/internet services, beers sold until 2am. **Prices** €20 for a single in a dorm, doubles €23, sheets €2.50 + €2.50 deposit, towels €1+ €1 deposit. **Web Site** www.woodstock.fr **Hot Nights/When to Go** Thursday-Saturday lots of young people hang out drinking here on the outdoor patio. **Close By** The Montmartre area…see the day review of *Sacre Coeur* for some specifics, but you'll find bars, restaurants, live music venues, laundry, and any facilities necessary in close proximity. The staff can lead you to anything you want.

Tip from Adam: "This is where I stay when I'm in Paris. Lots of young hippies are kickin' it here, and this area is home to so many music venues that I just can't stay anywhere else. Book ahead of time if you can, because this place gets packed."

OTHER

Café Oz

Bar	18 R. Saint Denis	Night
M-Th 3pm-2am, F-Sa 3pm-3am, Su 4pm-2am		

3 | 3 | 1 | 2

The Scene Good day mate, welcome to the Outback (not the steakhouse)! This is the feeling they try to convey to patrons at Café Oz. (Oz is the endearing nickname for the land down under, another nickname for Austrailia.) The bar, tables, and chairs are made of wood and look as if they were handmade. The décor is rich in Australian art and old photographs, depicting what past generations of Aussies did...drink at the pub. At night, however, they keep the place dark, lit only by funky black lights, which lends a funky vibe. **Crowd** A mix of French and English speakers. The crowd here is on the young side and very casual, as you would expect at a typical bar in the Outback.
Entertainment/Music There is a stage in the front of the bar that they use once in a while for live music, but mainly the entertainment is DJs who focus on rock. **Food/Misc** A giant fake crocodile greets you at the door. **Prices** Beers start at €5, cocktails start at €8, shots for €5; Happy hour every day 6-10pm: Cocktails €5, beers €4, and jugs for €13.
Web Site www.cafe-oz.com **Dress** Casual. **Hot Nights/When to Go** This place gets crowded, so if you want a table, which is the best idea, get here early (around 11pm).

Tip from Adam: "Reminds me of being in the Outback, without the 120 degree heat. But with a range of Aussie beers and a laid back vibe, a night here is fun and great to meet others who speak English."

China Club

Club	50 R. de Charenton	Night
Su-Th 7pm-2am, F-Sa 7pm-3am, closed in August		

3 | 4 | 3 | 3

The Scene This somewhat elegant, upscale bar/club has special appeal for jazz lovers, but with three diverse floors, it offers something for everyone, whatever your mood or taste. A striking black and white tile floor complements posh black leather sofas and elegant, huge, red velvet curtains. Bartenders in suits are a fitting and classy touch. The upstairs area makes the impression of an old man's den with Chinese paintings adorning the walls and a more tranquil feel. Head downstairs Thursday through Saturday nights to catch a live jazz performance in the swanky lounge. Although only the main floor serves appetizers to accompany your cocktails, the main restaurant is just next-door and has an extensive Asian menu. **Crowd** A well-dressed, well-groomed, and slightly sophisticated crowd in their mid-20s to mid-30s...many beautiful women. **Entertainment/Music** Live jazz Thursday-Saturday. During the week, they play different styles of jazz on each floor. **Food/Misc** Happy hour 6-9pm daily: all drinks are €6, including the martinis.
Prices Appetizers on the main floor €7-8 (spring rolls, dim sum), cocktails €9-11, beers €4-7. In the restaurant next door: main dishes €12-18, fixed menu €28. **Web Site** www.chinaclub.cc **Dress** Smart-Casual to dressy club attire. **Hot Nights/When to Go** Thursday through Saturday starting at happy hour (6-9pm).

Tip from Adam: "Come here on the weekend to catch some great, live jazz musicians. Head downstairs where there is another bar, and try to grab a spot on one of the comfy seats to mellow out and take in the music."

The Eiffel Tower

Culture		**Night**
Daily 9am-12am		Day

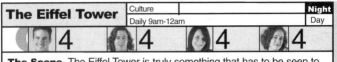

👤 4 👤 4 👤 4 👤 4

The Scene The Eiffel Tower is truly something that has to be seen to be fully appreciated, so make a night of it and have fun seeing this attraction. Right next to the tower is a park, which is an amazing place to set up a picnic late in the evening. Grab a sandwich and some bottles of wine with friends and find a place on the grass. As the sun sets, the tower becomes even more beautiful and illuminated with an orange glow. It is pretty sweet having dinner alongside one of the world's most famous attractions. After a nice dinner and some drinks, make your way to the top of the tower, either by stairs then elevator or the elevator all the way to the top, for the best views of Paris lit up under the night sky. **Crowd** In the park, hundreds of young French people enjoy a nice night. They drink wine, sing, and kick around the soccer ball. On the actual tower are thousands of tourists who don't want to miss the Eiffel Tower. **Food/Misc** There are a couple of restaurants on the tower itself, but if you are going up late, they will not be open. If you can't find wine, there are men walking around with bottles to sell. You can easily bargain with them. **Prices** €10.40 to the top in the elevator. €3.50 to take the stairs up to the second platform and then another €3.50 to take the elevator to the top. **Dress** Casual. **Hot Nights/ When to Go** This is something you can do any night of the week, but it is a great way to start off a Friday or Saturday of partying.

Tip from Emma: "If you want to save money, take the stairs to the second platform and then buy a ticket to get you to the top. Some travelers are known to bring their own refreshment to avoid the expensive drinks at the bar on the tower."

Fete de la Musique

Other		**Night**
June 21st		

👤 3 👤 4 👤 2 👤 4

The Scene Paris explodes with music on this night, as locals and tourists alike seem to set aside reality for the day and immerse themselves in carefree, impromptu music. A true celebration of our ability to create music, this party encourages music of all kinds, from percussion to Native American Folk music. The ambiance in the city is almost primitive, as thousands of people seem to relinquish themselves to the beat. Anything goes on this uniquely Parisian night, so be prepared to go with the flow and take advantage of the opportunity to meet many friendly and happy locals. Bars and streets remain spirited and busy all night and well into the morning with music seemingly coursing through the city's veins. **Crowd** Everyone in Paris seems to take part in this festival. The crowd is largely determined by the neighborhood. Younger people tend to enjoy the festival in 4eme and the Latin Quarter; you'll find them hanging out in the streets or packing the bars. Wherever you find yourself, it is sure to be packed with people simply enjoying themselves. **Entertainment/Music** Acts big and small play throughout the night. In fact, it seems as though anyone can set up a bongo and play. Lots of percussion and people doing the hippie-dance. **Food/Misc** Street vendors fill the streets throughout the city. So, finding quick food will not be a problem. **Prices** The festival is completely free.

Tip from Adam: "During this night, everyone is really friendly, so take advantage and meet new people. Chill out, listen to music, and take in a truly unique vibe. If you can make it, don't miss this party."

Le Sous Bock

Pub	49 R. St. Honore	**Night**
	Daily 11am-5am	

4 3 2 2

The Scene There is no question that they take their beers seriously here, as you can tell by the thousands of beer posters and coasters decorating the walls of this bar (as well as the 400 varieties of bottled beers they offer). A great late night stop for food and a huge choice of beers, Le Sous Block will probably remind you of the spot where you and your friends hang out drinking and playing darts back home. Although the name is French, the feel here is very much that of an American bar with an Irish influence. A fun and carefree atmosphere attracts a friendly International crowd. **Crowd** A young International crowd comes here to kick back and meet others. Very casual and fun people to be around. **Entertainment/Music** American style music generally, but don't be surprised if they change up the music to maintain an International flair. Also, there is a dartboard. **Food/Misc** They have a full menu consisting of lots of French food, but you can also enjoy fish and chips or some Irish stew. 400 bottled beers and 45 types of whiskey. **Prices** Appetizers start at €3, entrees start around €11, cocktails start at €6.10, and pints of beer start at €4.70.
Web Site www.sous.bock.com **Dress** Casual.
Hot Nights/When to Go Tuesday nights can be fun, but the weekends are most crowded. This place stays open late, so there will be other young people to meet late night.

Tip from Tuck: "With so many beers to choose from, I can come here all night and sample a little bit of flavor form every country. I love to hang out at the bar and then stir up a friend for a game of darts."

Parc des Buttes-Chaumont

	Other	
	Daytime hours	**Day**

3 3 3 4

The Scene Take the metro to this park on a sunny afternoon and set aside a few hours to relax in an amazing and picturesque environment. As in most parks, you'll find joggers, sunbathers, people walking their dogs, children playing, and more. Beyond that, however, Buttes-Chaumont offers a spectacular view of Paris and has a historic, stone-made gazebo atop a giant hill surrounded by a lake. You can cross a bridge onto this little island and hike up through steps in a cave to enjoy this romantic lookout point. The park is extremely scenic and offers plenty of trees/shade, as well rolling streams and small waterfalls leading to the central lake. **Crowd** People of all ages and types… a very friendly and social environment. **Entertainment/Music** Great paths for running/walking around the park. **Food/Misc** Food shack by the lake and water fountains throughout. **Dress** Completely casual.
Hot Nights/When to Go 7 days a week…park is most crowded on weekends. **Close By** Within the park, there are a variety of street performers and musicians. A shack by the lake sells crepes, waffles, sodas, ice cream, etc. for €2-5. *La Kascad,* at 2 place Armand Carrel offers lots of outdoor patio space with great views of the park, as well as a decent size indoor restaurant with a full menu. It is trendy with a Cuban theme. Many young, attractive people come here around happy hour for a drink and a smoke by the park.

Tip from Emma: "Whether you're looking to go for a jog, have some beers outside, or pick up a crepe and go for a stroll under the sun, this park is well worth your while."

Rex Club

Dance club	5 bd. Poissonniere	Night
Th-Sa 11:30pm - 6am (open some W nights as well…check website)		

👨 3   👩 2   👩 4   👩 2

PARIS OTHER

The Scene Rex gets some crazy DJs and live music, so be sure to check the website. The music and the dance floor are the heart and soul of this place, and you'll find a variety of funky music playing all the time. The live Hip-hop is absolutely insane, and patrons go nuts on the dance floor when the beat gets pumping. There are tables for the high-rollers who want to chill with their crew and a bottle of Bacardi. The stage is in the back with a packed dance floor in front of it. To the sides of the stage are small bars and more couches and tables on which to kick your feet up. Rex club is a late night venue for anyone looking to party hard all night long with live music, a hip crowd, crazy lights, and a friendly vibe. **Crowd** A young student crowd…20s and 30s…very hip, just trendy enough. They love hip-hop, drum and bass, techno, and all forms of groovy, powerful music. **Entertainment/ Music** House, techno, electro, drum n bass, hip-hop, reggae…something different and something special every night. **Prices** Free to €13 cover depending on who is performing or DJing. Bottles of premium alcohol about €120, mixed drinks €9, beers €6 and up. **Web Site** www.rexclub.com **Dress** Casual but stylish…club attire. **Hot Nights/ When to Go** Th-Sa around 2am.

Tip from Brittney: "This club rocks out hard every night, and the music is exotic and insane. Come here on a Friday or Saturday night when you are done with the bars and dance all night with this young, hip crowd."

Rue de Faubourg St. Honore

Other	
Daytime	Day

👨 1   👩 0   👩 4   👩 2

The Scene Ah Paris! The center of the fashion world obviously could not be complete without a street comprised of the most fashionable shops anywhere. Some you will recognize, and some are far too exclusive for anyone we know to recognize. Hermes, Pierre Cardin, Farragamo, and Prada (just to name a few) attract sophisticated shoppers. Lots of fancy jewelry, expensive art, and luxurious clothing lines the streets. Window shoppers abound here, but it's not a great place to meet young people. It is, however, a fun way to spend an hour or two exploring high fashion with a smaller crowd than on the Champs Elysées. **Crowd** The crowd here is generally older and has lots of money. Not a young persons' hangout. **Prices** Although it's free to walk the street, the stores here peddle some very expensive goods. **Dress** Smart casual. If you want to be treated well in the stores, you need to be a little dressed up to show you have cash to spend. **Close By** Just off the rue is *Buddha Bar*, a great place to get lunch and a cocktail in a tranquil setting. A variety of cafes and brasseries line the street. Eventually, this rue nears the Arc du Triumph, so when you see this, make your way over to the Champs-Elysées for plenty of places to hang out.

Tip from Brittney: "Put on nice clothes and take a walk along this street of beautiful fashion. Take the Metro to the Palais Royal du Louvre and start walking. Buying something here may be a little difficult to explain to your dad, but maybe those bonds from your uncle for your bat mitzvah finally matured."

Scala

Club	188 Bis R. de Rivoli		**Night**
Daily 10:30pm - 6am			

👤 3 👤 2 👤 3 👤 1

The Scene This late night dance club is open way past anyone's bedtime every night of the week; Scala is a place to let loose until the early morning sunshine. All sorts of flashing lights give the impression of staring at a Time's Square Billboard. This is, however, much more fun than that. Lively music sets the scene on a huge dance floor, and plenty of dark, secluded nooks both up and downstairs provide an opportunity to get to know someone a little better. Dancing here is frenzied and fun, and even though it is 2005, the "Macarena" is as loud and lively here as it was 10 years ago. Maybe you could just watch this from the bar. **Crowd** The crowd here is comprised of young people with nothing better to do than stay out dancing into the early morning. Lots of girls here who really like to dance and are good at it.

Entertainment/Music Primarily, Hip-hop and R&B, but they are also known to play some European music. **Prices** Cover charge is €12 and includes one drink at the bar. Other drinks are €9.

Dress Smart casual. **Hot Nights/When to Go** It is open every night of the week and is definitely a late night spot, so head here late when you want to keep the party going.

Tip from Tuck: "Late night during the week, like on a Wednesday, is good time to hit this spot. The cover may be expensive, but the strong drinks and the crowd are worth it. Don't miss the dance floor, because it's a great spot to meet girls who you can chat with later at a quieter table, even though you may not speak the same language."

Three Ducks
Travelers Hostel

Accomodation	6 Place Etienne Pernet	**Night**
		Day

👤 3 👤 3 👤 2 👤 3

The Scene This bar happens to also have beds to sleep in, so they call it a hostel. If you are looking for a good time and a short commute to the bar, then this is the place for you. The cheapest drinks in all of Paris keep the backpackers from ever having to leave the hostel to find a party. A rowdy time breaks out here just about every night of the week and even more so during the summer. A small patio behind the bar with one palm tree provides a great outdoor atmosphere for the middle of the city. This place has no trouble living up to its reputation as THE party hostel. The neighborhood surrounding Three Ducks is quiet and doesn't offer much in the way of nighttime entertainment. **Crowd** Many English-speakers frequent this hostel, especially Americans. Backpackers with only a couple of days in Paris love to come here to meet tons of people and party. **Food/Misc** They have a kitchen that is open 24 hours a day, but you have to supply your own groceries. **Prices** Bottles of red wine for €8 and €3.10 for a glass. Pint of beer for €3.50, bottles start at €2.90. Internet is €1 for every 15 minutes. Dorm beds are €23, triples for €25, and twins for €26 during the summer months. **Web Site** www.3ducks.fr **Dress** PJs. **Hot Nights/When to Go** Any night. **Close By** This hostel is located in a quiet neighborhood, so there is not much nightlife nearby. The Eiffel Tower is about a 10-minute walk, which might provide a diversion.

Tip from Tuck: "Great hostel to meet other people and have lots of fun. If you want to stay out all night, it's possible that they'll let you in at 6:30am, despite the 2am curfew."

UGC Cine	Movie	7 Place de la Rotonde	**Night**
Cite des Halles		Check movie times on line using French yahoo	Day

3 4 2 2

PARIS OTHER

The Scene The cinema experience here is much like in the US, with a few notable differences. Let us prepare you. The seats are probably the most posh and comfortable movie theater seats anywhere, and the movie will be preceded by about 15 minutes of French commercials peppered with a couple of previews. American movies will be in English with French subtitles. Don't be surprised by loud outbursts of commentary from some Frenchman; they really get into their movies over here. **Crowd** The movie determines the crowd, of course.
Food/Misc Concession stands offer popcorn, soda, and candy. You can either get popcorn with salt or sugar, and the soda comes with no ice, which means more soda and more trips to the bathroom.
Prices Normal ticket prices are €9, but show a student card for a €6.50 ticket. Popcorn and soda together are €5.50. **Dress** Casual.
Hot Nights/When to Go The best time to go the movies is on a Sunday night when you need to recover from the weekend.

Tip from Adam: "This is great way to get away from the bars. Going to a movie gives you the chance to get lost in your mind and to forget that you are in a foreign country. Don't worry if you get there late, because the stuff they show before the movie takes longer than in the States."